The Cats and the Water Bottles

Also by David Bouchier

The Song of Suburbia
The Accidental Immigrant
Radical Citizenship
The Feminist Challenge
Idealism and Revolution

The Cats and the Water Bottles

◆

and Other Mysteries of French Village Life

David Bouchier with illustrations by Diane Bouchier

ASJA Press
New York Lincoln Shanghai

The Cats and the Water Bottles
and Other Mysteries of French Village Life

All Rights Reserved © 2002 by David & Diane Bouchier

No part of this book may be reproduced or transmitted in any form or by any means, graphic, electronic, or mechanical, including photocopying, recording, taping, or by any information storage retrieval system, without the written permission of the publisher.

ASJA Press
an imprint of iUniverse, Inc.

For information address:
iUniverse
2021 Pine Lake Road, Suite 100
Lincoln, NE 68512
www.iuniverse.com

First published by Mid Atlantic Productions 2002

All personal names have been changed to protect the innocent. Any resemblance to real persons or cats, living or dead, is purely coincidental.

ISBN: 0-595-25337-7

Printed in the United States of America

To
Our friends in Aniane
For their patience

CONTENTS

PROLOGUE 1

Part I	VILLAGE LIFE
CHAPTER 1	First Impressions 7
CHAPTER 2	The Cats and the Water Bottles 15
CHAPTER 3	The Bells 17
CHAPTER 4	The Last of the Summer Wine 21
CHAPTER 5	Short Range Broadcasting 25
CHAPTER 6	Eating Dangerously 27
CHAPTER 7	The Mysterious Pies of Pézenas 33
CHAPTER 8	The Wonderful Invention of Monsieur Poubelle 37
CHAPTER 9	A Place on the Corner 39
CHAPTER 10	A Walk in the Country 43
CHAPTER 11	Safety Last 47
CHAPTER 12	Games of Chance 51
CHAPTER 13	The Circus Comes to Town 53
CHAPTER 14	Nothing is Easy 57
CHAPTER 15	Spoilt for Choice 61
CHAPTER 16	Living in the Past 63
CHAPTER 17	The Village Community 67

Part II — LANGUAGE PROBLEMS

CHAPTER 18	French as He is Spoke	73
CHAPTER 19	Hors de Combat	79

Part III — TRAVELS WITH A CITROEN

CHAPTER 20	Survival of the Fastest	83
CHAPTER 21	The Stevenson Trail	87
CHAPTER 22	The Memory Man	91
CHAPTER 23	The Tram to Odysseum	95
CHAPTER 24	Ship of Fools	99
CHAPTER 25	Who Loves Paris?	101
CHAPTER 26	A Modest Proposal	103
CHAPTER 27	Misguided Tours	105
CHAPTER 28	A Universal Language	109

Part IV — ADVENTURES IN FRENCH CULTURE

CHAPTER 29	Local Hero	113
CHAPTER 30	Long Live the Difference	117
CHAPTER 31	Love in a Warm Climate	121
CHAPTER 32	Toreador	125
CHAPTER 33	Loft Story	127
CHAPTER 34	Alternative Literature	129
CHAPTER 35	Strike of the Day	133
CHAPTER 36	Bastille Day	137

PROLOGUE

It seems that everyone dreams about spending a year in France, or perhaps in Italy. This is the fault of Peter Mayle, whose charming and enormously successful 1989 book *A Year in Provence* told the story of his family's adventures moving into a house in a village in the south of France. It sounded idyllic and wonderful although, soon after he published *A Year in Provence*, Mayle moved to the even more idyllic and wonderful territory of Long Island.

Since Peter Mayle hit the publishing jackpot, there has been a deluge of books based on the same romance—a year in France, a year in Tuscany, and so on. These stories have some similarities. The setting is extraordinarily picturesque. The voluntary exiles buy an old farmhouse or château, and go through a painful period of restoration, decoration, finding the right contractors, trouble with the plumbing and the servants and the swimming pool. They spend millions of dollars, but it is worth it in the end.

I love reading these books. They are what I call travel pornography. But everybody's experience of France is different. We rejected the idea of buying a château. Instead we rented a small house in an unfashionable village in an unfashionable region, where we had a wonderful time. The pool and the servants were not a problem.

The village was in the region called Languedoc, down towards the Spanish border. Languedoc is not like Provence. Aniane is nothing like Peter Mayle's Ménèbres.

These essays were originally broadcast weekly on National Public Radio Stations WSHU and WSUF in Connecticut and Long Island. A selection is also available on audio as a two-CD set called "Letters from France."

I would like to acknowledge the invaluable editorial help of Eléonore M. Zimmermann who read the manuscript from a French viewpoint and corrected many errors of fact and interpretation. The mistakes that remain are entirely my own invention.

The person who made this trip possible was my wife Diane, who decided to use her university sabbatical in this creative way instead of spending a year in the library. She also generously agreed to take me along, and to illustrate these pages with her entertaining sketches, taken almost directly from life.

Part I

Village Life

1

First Impressions

Aniane has no superficial charm, but plenty of character. It was founded, according to legend, in the year 777 and survives as an almost-intact medieval village with about fifteen hundred inhabitants and no parking space. There is no record of the earliest structures, but maps and sketches from five hundred years ago show the street pattern and many of the buildings virtually as they are now. It always gave us a thrill to imagine that people walked these same narrow streets five centuries ago, grumbling about the weather and the dogs, and speaking the ancient language of Occitan, as they still do.

Like any new immigrants, we arrived with many anxieties. How would we live here, so far from the familiar culture and comforts of Long Island? Would we be able to manage life's basic survival tasks like understanding the TV schedule, making friends with the neighborhood cats, and finding a bakery that had really good croissants? This is a good example of how we always worry about the wrong things. Croissants were not a problem: there was a bakery at each end of our street. The TV was so exceptionally bad that the schedule was irrelevant, and the local cats were rather more friendly than was strictly necessary.

September is a month of great changes in the South of France. The weather is still mostly beautiful, but showing ominous hints of the rainy, windy autumn just ahead. Virtually all the summer visitors are heading home. The roads are jammed with millions of French, German, British and Scandinavian sun worshippers, returning to their schools and their jobs, reluctantly abandoning this southern playground. The tourist season is over. From the Riviera to Provence, and even in our less fashionable region of Languedoc, there is an almost audible collective sigh of relief from the people who actually live down there year round.

They call this period the *arrière-saison*—literally the back of the season. It is a true autumn—economic, spiritual, meteorological, and biological. Most of the restaurants and tourist spots are still open at the beginning of September. But during the next few weeks they close one by one. Even the shops will cut down on their opening hours, and the owners will retire to their winter homes in Spain, or former French Africa, or even in some cases Florida or Cuba. They'll be back in April.

Meanwhile, we had only just arrived. Our neighbors found this amazing, and almost perverse, like moving into your summer place in the Hamptons just after Labor Day. They were too polite to ask directly why on earth were we there, why we had chosen to live in a village house, and what on earth we were going to do with ourselves through the winter.

We were asking the same questions. We knew that life in such a village would be different, but we hadn't quite realized *how* different. For example we had to get accustomed to a lot less personal space. When you have lived in the American suburbs for a while, you take it for granted that everyone has plenty of space. Wide streets, big sprawling houses, half-acre gardens, and double or quadruple garages seem entirely normal. A medieval village in the south of France was not the same.

Aniane was a maze of narrow streets, some of them scarcely more than alleyways. Our street, Rue de la tour or Street of the tower was exactly 180 centimeters or 71 inches wide—I measured it. It was just barely possible to drive a small car into the street. But as I discovered, much to the amusement of the neighbors, it was almost impossible to back it out again because of the tight turns. This guaranteed that there was virtually no motor traffic in the center of the village, and therefore no traffic noise. Parking was a nightmare or a challenge, depending on how you looked at it. After a few weeks of living there, my definition of a "parking space" became more and more elastic. I soon gave up the idea of finding a neat little box marked out by white lines. Any scrap of sidewalk without a cat sleeping on it was a parking space. The triangular corner behind the garbage cans beside the river was a parking space. The spot between the fountain and the church door was a parking space, if I was lucky enough to get it.

The fact that the village architecture discouraged motor vehicles had many advantages. When you can't drive up to your own front door, shopping is drastically limited. There's no point loading up the car at the supermarket in the next town, because every item has to be carried through a quarter of a mile of narrow streets. It was easier to use the village shops. Everything of importance was right on our doorstep: three bakers, a butcher, a farm shop, several wineries, two grocers, a drugstore, and a market every Thursday.

Miscellaneous purchases, like flashlight batteries and an ironing board, led us down a narrow alleyway to the amazing, un-advertised emporium of Monsieur Vidal. The cliché about Aladdin's Cave has been overworked, but in the case of Monsieur Vidal's store, no other cliché will do. He had everything, or he would get it for you next day—whether a bottle of barbecue lighting fluid or a packet of computer disks. Everybody came here, and the gnome-like Monsieur Vidal assisted by his slightly mad poodle Bruno orchestrated the shopping needs of the village like air traffic controllers at a busy airport. He also delivered bottled gas personally, which you will realize is no small matter when I tell you about the stairs. His opening and closing schedule was completely arbitrary, and unknown even to the locals. Customers would peer down the narrow alley to see if Vidal's battered car was there, or the plastic basket that he sometimes remembered to hang out as an "open" sign. If not, they would shrug and carry on.

The original builders of Aniane had no interest in wide boulevards for convenient shopping, but they did like to build *upwards* for security against invading Saracens, Moors, Spaniards and, more recently, tourists.

In the old days, cattle lived on the lowest floor of the houses, and hay was kept in the attics to be dropped down to the animals through a shaft. The family lived on the middle two floors, presumably with bales of hay whizzing past their ears. Our house wasn't as wide as an American double garage, but it was four stories tall. The front door was three feet above the level of the street, and that was just the beginning. The rooms were high, and the stairs were steep. In the first few weeks, we spent a lot of time gasping for breath.

All this climbing had a health payoff. If we wanted this kind of workout in America we would have to buy one of those exercise machines called a Stairmaster. But we built leg muscles like Olympic athletes just by living in Aniane. Also, the ordinary temptations of daily life were much reduced. When you have your first *apéritif* on the top floor terrace, and the bottle is in the kitchen down two steep flights of stairs, you're likely to settle for just admiring the view.

We necessarily lived close to our neighbors on all sides. They were on top of us, and we were on top of them. There were no suburban open spaces to soften our togetherness. The walls of the houses were thick, and made of solid granite: but the windows were open. So we got to know people, through their family conversations and cooking smells, as well as by the inescapable encounters in the narrow street. It worked very well. Everyone kept their voices low, nobody played loud music, and the after-lunch siesta hour was more or less sacred.

Laundry was an important part of this public/private life. Very few village houses had dryers, and not many had back yards. So the only place to hang your wet laundry was out the front window. This gave the streets a festive air on a sunny day, and created a harmless competition between the housewives (who still exist there) over the quantity, the quality and the frequency of their washing. Young widows could also use this public forum for a bit of discreet advertising—some surprisingly filmy garments were on display—and the presence or absence of hanging laundry was a very good indication of the day's weather. Abundant laundry meant that it would stay dry, and it would be a good day for a trip. The housewives were almost never wrong, and considerably more accurate than the official weather forecast.

The central social space in the village used to be the public washing tubs behind the chapel. Now that everyone has running water, the action has shifted to the hairdressing salon beside the town hall. My wife Diane and I both patronized this useful establishment, but we felt a bit conspicuous. The windows allowed every passer-by to look in, which they did, and many people came in for conversation, or to suggest hairstyle improvements to whoever happened to be in the chair at the time. These were usually on the lines of "More Henna," because flaming red hair was very much the fashion with women of all ages. Monsieur Vidal spent more time there than in his own general store up the street. Everyone knew that if Monsieur Vidal was dispensing coffee and gossip at the hairdresser's, his own shop must be closed. The general effect was of being in a fishbowl with a lot of friendly but unfamiliar fish.

As in any French village, there was an enormous amount of talk. Everyone seemed to know everyone else, and they held intense, loud and apparently continuous discussions in the street, the post office, the *tabac*, and the hairdressers. They had no need of cellular phones.

What they were saying was another matter. There was, to put it mildly, a regional accent. All languages have regional accents, of course. Generally speaking, the farther south you travel the more incomprehensible the accent becomes. If you've been to the American deep south, you know what I mean. Britain is a rare exception to this rule, its most peculiar accents being found in the far north. But France is not. The south is another country, they say things differently there.

This had me worried at first. My French is pretty bad, but I can usually manage an ordinary conversation. Here, standing in the market or the post office, I understood nothing. I might as well have been in Mississippi, or Scotland.

This linguistic incompetence was explained when I learned a little more about the history of the region. It is called Languedoc, which is a corruption of the phrase "Langue d'Oc," or language of Oc. Back in the early middle ages, this part of France spoke a unique language, Occitan, derived from Latin and completely different from the French spoken in the north. In fact the linguistic division was based on those who said "oc" for "oui" (southerners) and those who said something like "oil" (northerners). Generations later it was clear to me that the old way of speech still survived in the south. These people weren't speaking French, they were speaking Oc. No wonder I couldn't understand them. I always had trouble with Latin at school, and finally dropped out of the class after a long series of Fs.

Diane said that I was fooling myself, and that the language problem was all in my head. Her French was admittedly much better than mine. When she went shopping she often came back with the right things, whereas I did not. But I was convinced that, as soon as I could find an English-Oc dictionary my problems would be solved. When the tourists came flocking back in the spring I planned to be speaking Oc like a native. However, because it is such an ancient and subtle language, I didn't necessarily expect to be understood.

2

The Cats and the Water Bottles

"This village is overpopulated with cats," said our new landlord, only minutes after we arrived in Aniane. We were astonished by this news. We had never imagined that any place *could* be overpopulated with cats. Too many human beings are always a problem, but surely you can never have too many cats?

There certainly were a lot of cats in Aniane. They slept in the gutters, walked down the middle of the narrow streets, and peered down from windows and balconies. The tiled roofs of the village, which were virtually all connected, provided a huge exclusive cat territory: on a sunny day, every roof had a cat on it. It was impossible to avoid close encounters of the furred kind. Our first feline visitor, Monsieur Alphonse, jumped over the wall within three minutes of our arrival. This was a cat-lovers' paradise.

The cats of Aniane have created for themselves a village version of an urban legend, which I will try to explain.

We noticed immediately that many houses had two large bottles of spring water on the doorstep, one bottle on each side. It might be Vittel, or Evian, or any of the popular brands. The bottles on our doorstep contained Ogeu spring water from the Pyrénées mountains, although it turned out that this had no special significance.

At first we assumed that it was some kind of house-to-house delivery service. The British take it for granted that bottles of milk are delivered to their doorsteps every day, and this must be the French equivalent.

Our neighbor Chantal explained that this, like all our other interpretations of French culture, was wrong. The bottles of water were there to discourage the cats, who would otherwise use the doorways for unauthorized and unsanitary purposes, which in turn would cause the wooden doors to rot and fall apart, at great expense to the homeowners.

We could scarcely believe this explanation. Never in a lifetime of owning and observing cats have we seen any one of them behaving in such an antisocial way. Dogs, yes, but dogs are dogs, and have their own ways of expressing their opinions. More evidence was produced. Chantal pointed out the defensive boards. Those houses that didn't have bottles in front of their doors had stout boards, about a foot high. They looked like barriers against flooding. But our street was way above the level of the river and, short of another deluge of forty days and forty nights, we could never be flooded. The boards, like the bottles, were a defense against the wicked cats.

Other villages in the area had plenty of cats, but no water bottles or boards. Admittedly, they had plenty of rotting doors, but that's because wooden doors *do* tend to rot from the bottom up, especially if they are more than a hundred years old.

Frankly, we didn't know what to make of this legend about cats, water bottles and doors. If rotting doors had to be blamed on somebody, the finger pointed straight at the dogs of Aniane. They were as numerous as the cats and, unlike the cats, they left their traces everywhere. But the French absolutely adore and worship their dogs. Dogs cannot be blamed for anything. Everything must be the fault of the wretched cats.

On the other hand, perhaps we were the victims here. Whenever newcomers appear in a village, it's tempting to tell them tall stories about the local culture. I've done it myself, when I lived in a small English village. Even great anthropologists like Malinowski and Margaret Mead, trying to understand alien customs, found themselves at the mercy of playful locals who knew how to tell a good tale. They repeated it all in good faith, just as I have told you the story of the water bottles and the cats.

Which left us with the question: what *were* those bottles doing there, and what would become of us if we removed them from the doorstep?

3

The Bells

Soon after we arrived in France I stopped wearing a watch. This was quite a dramatic decision, for me. Over several decades my left wrist had developed a permanent circular indentation, from the constant pressure of a watch strap, and my brain had been similarly dented by the constant pressure of deadlines and appointments. This year, I decided to let time take care of itself.

Things are never that simple. It's impossible to escape the tyranny of time. Most villages in France maintain one or more public clocks, usually in the tower of the main church or the town hall. Public clocks are easy to ignore, unless they chime.

If you have ever lain awake at night in a European hotel room, listening to the relentless progression of the hours, you know exactly what I mean. These chimes are not apologetic little tinkles, like the ones you get from your bedside alarm clock; they ring out across the whole village.

There was only one chiming clock, in the tower of the Chapel of the Penitents. But this just happened to be fifty yards from our house. The first night we spent there we thought that we would have to go without sleep the whole year. After a while we scarcely noticed the bells at all. When we did hear them they told us what time it was *not*.

The chiming clock of Aniane had two endearing faults. The first was that it rang every hour and half hour twice. At first, we assumed that these were two different clocks, chiming out of sequence. But no, it was one clock, chiming twice. This was a wonderful service for the half-witted and half-asleep. If you missed the time the first time, you could always get the time the second time, which might be up to ten minutes later.

The other charming fact about this clock was that it was almost never right on either set of chimes. Before I stopped wearing my watch, I noticed that the church clock rang at approximately nine minutes before and three minutes after the hour, and the same on the half hour. Then it caught up, until the first set of chimes was exactly right for a day or two, and then it slowly drifted off again.

The church of Saint Sauveur, which was on the other side of our house and even closer, also had a bell which was not connected to a clock. It rang a random number of strokes at unpredictable times, just to keep everybody on their toes.

This was a refreshing change from our time-obsessed American culture. The day had the same number of hours in it whether we knew the exact time or not. In fact, days in Aniane seemed to have rather more hours than were strictly necessary. Before we left home our agenda books were crammed full of activities and commitments. Now the pages were alarmingly empty, except for lists of opening and closing times. The village shops were geared to the church clock, rather than to the atomic clock in Colorado, and followed a mysterious weekly timetable known only to locals of the fifth generation. On Mondays the butcher was closed, but the hairdresser might or might not open at 2.15, or perhaps 3.52 if she visited her mother first, and depending on when the clock struck. On Tuesdays the fish stall would be in the square some time between 8 and 10 a.m., but this was also the day that Mr. Vidal would close the general store for the afternoon at around noon, or not, depending on whether he had orders to collect in Montpellier. Everyone took a long break in the middle of the day, and some stores opened only once a week. We tried to compile a timetable that would include all these factors but, like a complex multivariate analysis, it was never accurate or complete. In fact, the times scarcely mattered. You could walk across the whole village in five minutes to see what was open. This anticipatory shopping became as much of a ritual as shopping itself.

The French attitude to time is subtly different from ours, and the nuances are hard to grasp. French people in general are very relaxed about meetings and deadlines, but they are never relaxed on the road. Their trains are among the most punctual in the world, and everyone is obsessively prompt for meals. But they always seem to make time for conversation, no matter what other urgent business may be going on.

I like to imagine that the wine industry, which is the mainstay of the economy in Languedoc, has a benign influence on how people see and use time. It takes patience to make good wine, and optimism about the future. Above all, you must not be in a hurry. It's a great gift not to be in a hurry.

4

The Last of the Summer Wine

Driving through parts of southern France you could imagine yourself in California, or on the east end of Long Island. It's not just the overpriced restaurants that give this impression, but the vines. The village of Aniane lay in the heart of the region called Languedoc, a historic winegrowing area. Vines were everywhere, and they made a pleasing landscape. In November they produced a brilliantly colorful effect, like fall in New England except that all the foliage was at waist level. The wine industry, unlike most others, creates beauty as a by-product.

As temporary residents we felt a moral obligation to support this important local industry. So we made a habit of visiting the nearby vineyards. Most of them offered wine for sale directly to the public, and many advertised "Tastings." But their sales techniques fell far short of what we were accustomed to in America.

Wineries in Languedoc are not cute. On Long Island, as in California, our wineries are styled like country estates or post-modern châteaux, with well-designed and seductive tasting rooms. Around Aniane, most wineries looked like exactly what they are: factories. If you are lucky enough to find one open at the advertised time, you walk into a plain concrete building full of plastic and vats and humming machinery. They are not expecting company, least of all strange foreigners wanting to buy wine. But someone, often the proprietor, will pour a glass or two out of courtesy. However, there's no guarantee that you will actually be allowed to buy any.

Never mind the official categories and appellations, there are really two kinds of wine: those that the vintners care about, and those they don't. There's an ocean of cheap, mass-produced wine in this part of France, stuff that you buy at the supermarket or pump by the liter into plastic containers, like gasoline. In fact, it is slightly cheaper than gasoline. Then there are the special wines, carefully created from superior blends of grapes, grown in a particular territory, and produced in limited quantities.

The Rubaiyat of Omar Khayyam has these poignant lines:
"I often wonder what the vintners buy
One half so precious as the goods they sell."
The answer is that, if it's *that* precious, they simply don't sell it.
Late in the year after the end of the harvest, the usual response to a request for one of these special wines was:
"Sorry, none left."

To be polite, and to get rid of us, the winemakers often sent us off to a retail outlet, where the answer was: "None left." In one memorable case, when we were in hot pursuit of a rare white wine from last year's harvest, we were sent from one place to another, and finally to a Monsieur Rannou in a distant village who, we were told, might have some in his garage.

"None left," said Monsieur Rannou, peering out of his half-open garage door like a suspicious tortoise. When pressed, he reluctantly admitted that he might have two or three bottles of that wine, hidden behind a pile of old tires in the darkness at the back. Eventually we were grudgingly allowed to buy six, for cash.

The Romans pioneered this sales technique four thousand years ago. They kept all the best wine for Roman citizens, and sent the rubbish to the colonies. As a result, colonists were willing to pay almost any amount to get their hands on the good stuff. It worked for me. If they didn't want to sell it, I *really* wanted to buy it.

Our closest local vineyard in Aniane was more generous than the average. When we walked in, the proprietor and his dog were *tête à tête* with several friends.

"None left," they said, automatically. But when they learned that we were actually living here through next year, and that Diane at least was a bit of a connoisseur, they cheerfully sold us twelve bottles—plus one thrown in for free.

Wine is an important commodity in France, and also something more. Vines have been grown around here for almost four thousand years, and the process of making wine is no quicker now that it was then. We visited a handsome cellar, originally dug by the Romans, in which long rows of oak barrels contained the vintages of the last seven years, slowly maturing. When bottled, they may take another ten or twenty years to reach their peak. You or somebody you love must wait many years for this treat. Grandfathers still lay down wine for their infant grandsons and grand daughters to enjoy decades later. People who work in this industry know how to wait. Instant gratification is not the name of their game.

5

Short Range Broadcasting

Aniane had a lively gossip network. Just about everything important could be learned by hanging around in the Post Office, the hairdressing salon, or Monsieur Vidal's general store. But the village also had its own short-range radio station that could be heard for about half a mile in every direction. It wasn't a radio station in the technical sense. It had no frequency or transmitter, and needed no receiver. You received it whether you wanted to or not.

At the center of the village, the Romanesque tower of the 12th century church of The Penitents carried an incongruous array of powerful loudspeakers.

Fortunately we were warned about this by our landlord, who had no doubt lost many good tenants to heart attacks when the loudspeakers went into action. They did this at about ten o'clock every morning, and unpredictably in the late afternoon. The broadcast was signaled by a blast of music. It may be Mozart, or a fanfare of trumpets, or a pop tune. During our first few weeks, the village DJ had taken to playing a few bars from an old hit by Little Richard, called "Tutti Frutti."

If you were quietly reading, or contemplating the sublime landscape from your balcony, this could be a rude shock. But, having jolted the good people of Aniane into a semblance of alertness, the DJ went on to give the local news. This was local news indeed! A death or a funeral might be announced, with solemn music, or an appeal for the return of a lost dog or, on Thursdays, highlights of the weekly open-air market.

"The fishmonger had fresh tuna and octopus today; Madame Léfarge had a selection of five goat's cheeses from her farm; there is a special offer on olive oil from the establishment of Monsieur Bernard." These announcements were a signal to drop whatever you were doing and head to the market, which was only three minutes away. Everybody else was heading there too and, if you sat about wondering whether you actually *wanted* any goat's cheese, it would all be gone.

The Aniane village DJ also announced church services, sporting events, and meetings of the local Communist Party. During the gas crisis he told us what we already knew, that there was no gas, and he offered useful warnings, such as: "Your water supply will be cut off in ten minutes." On the rare occasions when the local branch library opened for an hour or two, he announced this too.

The identity of the village DJ remained a mystery. Like a Muzzein in his tower, he was the disembodied voice of the community, calling us to our daily tasks, and reminding us of our duties.

The whole broadcast was over in less than five minutes and, after a valedictory blast of music, the speakers fell silent. No commentary, no analysis: as they used to say in the old police dramas, just the facts. The village DJ, whoever he was, had the kind of job that every broadcaster dreams about. He was always finished in time for lunch and, short of dynamiting the church tower, his audience could never turn him off.

However, no public service is without its dark side. The messages that boomed out over Aniane were not always as clear as they should be, especially on windy days. From time to time, there was a long, apparently urgent announcement of which we did not understand a single word. Then we spent the rest of the day worrying about what we might have missed.

6

Eating Dangerously

Napoleon, who changed so many things in France, had no influence whatsoever on French eating habits. He believed that meals were just an annoying interruption of the business of conquest, and should be over in ten minutes. He died of a stomach disorder. Nobody has forgotten this.

Food and health are two of the great French obsessions. Before we came to France, I never thought about my liver, any more than I thought about the correct way to make a fish stock. After being there for a couple of months, both these things were constantly on my mind.

French food has an undeserved reputation for being unhealthy. It's true that some regions, like Burgundy, have cuisines that seem positively suicidal. But, if statistics mean anything, the French diet is one of the healthiest in the world. Heart attacks kill three times as many people in the United States as they do in France. This is called the "French Paradox," and health experts can't agree on the reason for it. At one time, all the credit was given to red wine: a bottle a day keeps *le médecin* away. New research has thrown doubt on this. Rather disappointingly, the evidence now suggests that the French simply eat less, and eat better. Most people eat only one major meal per day, they don't snack between meals, and their diet includes a lot of fish, plenty of fresh fruit and vegetables, always a green salad, and very little meat. In other words, it's the same sad story that nutritionists have been telling us for decades.

In addition to eating less, and better, the French eat much more slowly than Americans. A good dinner, like a good lunch, includes three, four or five courses, and takes about three hours. This prompted my brother-in-law Dennis, when he was visiting from Washington DC, to make the following joke.

Q: Why don't the French eat snacks between meals?

A: There's no time.

Of course, health is always a matter of swings and roundabouts, Yin and Yang. What the French gain in lifespan from their good eating habits is more than cancelled out by their horrific level of traffic accidents, and their insistence on smoking vile cigarettes everywhere and all the time. So the health benefits of a meal in a French restaurant are finely balanced. On the one hand the ingredients are excellent, and the slow pace is good for you. On the other, you will inhale a lot of smoke. In one popular local restaurant we were almost asphyxiated by the combined effects of a huge wood fire, where trout and lamb were being barbequed indoors, and dozens of strong cigarettes being puffed by the diners. The room was literally filled with smoke, as if the building was on fire. The customers, including babies, were rubbing their eyes and coughing. But, between paroxysms, they carried on eating without missing a beat.

We met many animals in French restaurants, usually cats and dogs, who could often be persuaded to share our meal. For anyone brought up with American habits of food hygiene, the happy companionship of humans and animals at the dinner table can be something of a shock. But it is a companionship that dates back several million years, and it reminds us of the basic pleasures that we share with our fellow-travelers on the evolutionary roller coaster.

Dining out in people's homes was more challenging. Quite apart from the problems of language and accent, we just didn't know the rules. One thing we learned is: never turn up with wine, unless you happen to own a vineyard and have something special to share. Everyone has an ocean of wine already.

It was also disconcerting to discover that the French still practice the archaic art of dinner conversation. Children and foreigners were expected to participate to the best of their abilities. Every meal was like a seminar, with topics being handed around the table. Just to make things more tense, and despite the interminable length of meals, it was not considered good manners use the bathroom in somebody else's house. For men of a certain age, this restriction can be uncomfortable to say the least, and it is in sharp contrast to American dinner etiquette, which requires every guest to visit the bathroom at least once in order to admire the fittings.

We ate a lot of our meals in local restaurants. Contrary to myth, French restaurants can be very bad. Some popular brasseries and tourist restaurants offer food as disgusting as anything you can find in America, and the waiters aren't even nice to you. They never say: "Hi, I'm Jacques, I will be your server today." They say as little as possible, and most of their remarks are *sotto voce* insults. In 2002, the French government launched a campaign to persuade French waiters to be nicer to their customers. The results are not yet in.

There are so many restaurants in France that tourists, who don't have much time, are almost forced to trust a guidebook. We have always used the Red Guide—the former Michelin Guide—that has been the Bible French travelers and tourists since 1900. It is, quite simply, an independent guide to restaurants and hotels in all of France—which means, of course, that there's nothing simple about it.

In the choice of hotels, this guide had never let me down. However modest your budget, the Red Guide will pinpoint exactly the right resting place. This is accomplished with the aid of a complicated code of symbols. In the early days, they often indicated certain inconveniences, such as the absence of electricity, or running water, in your chosen hotel. Now, the symbols promise the traveler all kinds of luxuries, such as air conditioning, Jacuzzis, and special facilities for dogs. The system isn't perfect, of course. There is no warning symbol if your picturesque country hotel is right next to a giant traffic intersection, or under the flight path of the French Air Force, or the meeting place for the local rugby club.

In each annual edition of the Red Guide, some hotels are upgraded or downgraded, added or deleted, with very little fuss. It's the restaurant ratings, and especially those at the top of the scale, that capture the attention of the French.

Selected restaurants are classified with one to five crossed knives and forks. At the low end of the scale, a single knife and fork guarantees that you will probably get some cutlery. For particularly fine cuisine, restaurants receive the distinction of one, two or three stars. Only twenty-one establishments in the whole country have three stars. However, if you can't get a reservation at one of these there are 760 McDonalds in France with no stars, and no reservations. The big news for gourmets in 2001 was that the celebrity chef Marc Veyrat in Savoie had won the very great honor of three stars for each of his two restaurants, while chef Alain Ducasse had lost one star for his restaurant in Monaco.

This report created hysteria and hypertension in the world of *haute cuisine*, but it left us totally unmoved. Unless we win the lottery, we're never likely to eat in any of these establishments. A couple of years ago, in a moment of mad extravagance, we dined at a one star restaurant near Paris. It was all theater and not much substance. There are only so many things you can do with meat and potatoes, and we almost had to take out a second mortgage to pay the card bill.

We wouldn't travel in France without our Red Guide, but the fact is that there are many thousands of fine eating places not listed, if only you have the time and patience and intestinal fortitude to seek them out. My personal, secret test of a French restaurant is entirely external. It must be painted brown, and have a front window divided into square panes, covered with a net curtain. This test has served me well for over forty years.

Our favorite village restaurant fit these criteria perfectly. It was a hole in the wall about the size of an American suburban garage, and served excellent food with local ingredients and local wines. This was a "Family

Restaurant" which means something slightly different in France. It is a bit like eating with the family insofar as they are often right there at the next table, and you feel obliged to eat more than you want because of guilt. ("We just cooked this specially today…") *La Moustardière* offered charming service, good food, and very modest prices. But it didn't have even a single crossed knife and fork in the Red Guide, or even a toothpick. In restaurants, as in love, it is necessary sometimes to trust one's own judgment.

7

The Mysterious Pies of Pézenas

Despite of the fact that McDonald's has almost eight hundred flourishing outlets in France and that pizza has become the universal diet of the younger generation, real food is still important there. There are thousands of old-fashioned local specialties to be enjoyed by the bold or foolhardy visitor.

This region of Languedoc-Roussilon has a relatively simple cuisine because the area has never been wealthy. It relies heavily on olive oil and garlic. For example the town of Castelnaudary is famous for its white beans. When combined with goose grease, lard and miscellaneous scraps of pork, lamb, duck and sausage, and cooked for about a week, these beans become the celebrated dish *Cassoulet* which is delicious, although not recommended for the digestively challenged. The handsome city of Sète, down on the Mediterranean, is known for its savoury fish stew with aioli, the *Bourride*, and also for *Seiche*, a white, rubbery mollusk that tastes just like white rubber until you put some kind of sauce on it. *Oulade* is made with potatoes and seasoned with pickled pork and herbs. *Aligot* is a delicious purée of potatoes, cheese and garlic, cream and butter. It would be easy and very pleasant to eat yourself to death in Languedoc.

In addition to these well-known regional recipes, almost every town and village promotes a particular item of food or drink, grown or made locally. These are sometimes sold in tourist shops, as souvenirs. But they have the great advantage that you don't have to carry them home and live with them—you can just eat or drink your souvenir, and carry home the queasy memory of it. I don't know if the locals ever eat these local specialties themselves, but I doubt it.

Here are a few of the things we tried. I hope my doctor doesn't read this.

We've sampled the orange brioches and the ancient *tripes* of Béziers (though not at the same time); the famous oysters of Bouzigues; the sweet almond calissons of Aix; the rum-flavored sausages of Lunel; the citron biscuits of Bédarieux; the flavored honeys of Roquebrun; the grilled anchovies of Nimes; *Cargolade* or barbecued snails, from the south; *Confit de canard* in west; *Brandade de morue* (salt cod puréed with garlic, olive oil and milk); *Seiche* stuffed with sausage; and the wild boar terrine of Roujon. At Le Puy en Velay, we tried and later regretted their pungent green liqueur called *Verveine* and, over a period of time, we tasted a creditable number of the several hundred local wines.

Many of these gastronomic treats come with a history, purporting to explain their connection with a particular place. For example: *Pélardon* goat's cheese is said to have been created in the Cevennes by an Abbot called Boissier de Sauvages in 1756, presumably with the help of a few goats. But I suspect that these histories are flights of fancy, dreamed up by the local tourist office during the dark days of February. Along with everything else in Europe these days, local food specialties are almost certainly regulated by the European Community in Brussels, which allocates one gourmet delight to each locality. This way there's no unfair competition, and every town gets the specialty it deserves.

We were particularly intrigued by the unusual food item assigned to a town called Pézenas, not far from Aniane. This charming town was once the unofficial capital of the region, and the home of Molière. The local gastronomic treats were small, round pies about an inch and a half across and two inches high, unimaginatively called "The Pies of Pézenas." The story is this. In 1766 (or 1767 or 1768, depending on which book you read), an English nobleman called Lord Clive (or Olive, or Clyde, depending on which book you read) came to Pézenas for his health, bringing with him an Indian cook, because he didn't trust the French cuisine. This cook prepared, among other things, some curried sweet meat pies (*petites pâtés*, filled with a kind of curry consommé) for picnics on the river. When Lord Clive (or Olive or Clyde) departed he passed on the secret recipe to the grateful citizen of Pézenas, who have been making the pies and selling them to unsuspecting tourists ever since.

As stories go, this one is a winner. I suppose it's just possible that the celebrated governor of India, Lord Clive, did pass this way. I suppose that he, or his Indian cook, might have left this recipe behind as a joke, assuming that either of them had a sense of humor, or perhaps even as a payback for some insult suffered at the hands of the locals. Whatever the truth of the matter, the curried sweet meat pies of Pézenas are a unique gastronomic experience. When I took some along to share with my French class they were a sensation.

The bureaucrats of the European Community have not yet got around to allocating a tasty treat to Aniane. We have some suggestions, and even some recipes. But, like Lord Clive, we're keeping them to ourselves until we are quite certain that we won't be going back.

8

The Wonderful Invention of Monsieur Poubelle

The history of human evolution is the history of garbage disposal. Our earliest ancestors tossed their rubbish into the back of the cave. When they ran out of space, they found a new cave. All through the slow climb towards civilization, human garbage was treated with no respect—emptied out of windows with little regard to passing traffic, piled up behind houses or thrown over the walls of castles. These unsanitary habits provided a treasure house for present-day archaeologists. But they didn't do much to improve the environment at the time. Most towns, villages, and cities were full of stinking garbage.

Civilization really began with the professionalization of garbage in nineteenth century France. Most Americans, as they trundle their bins out into the cold dawn, don't realize that they owe this convenience to a famous Frenchman, Monsieur Eugène-René Poubelle (1833-1907). This convivial, multi-talented man was a historical figure in more ways than one. As a professor of law and a radical democrat, he was suspected of treason by Napoleon III. But he survived, and after the fall of the Empire, M. Poubelle was appointed Prefect (or Governor) of the Paris region, where he made many improvements in architecture and public services.

But the thing he really wanted to do was clean the place up. Not to put too fine a point on it, Paris was a filthy city. In 1884, Prefect Poubelle introduced a law that required each homeowner to provide a special bin for garbage, which was then collected at regular intervals by carts which traveled around the city, announcing their arrival with blasts on a hunting horn. Nobody had proposed such a simple and radical reform since the foundation of Paris some two thousand years before. Proper garbage collection had arrived, and it was enormously popular with the citizens, who made M. Poubelle into a kind of hero.

The original garbage cans were round, and made of galvanized iron. The modern French version is square and plastic. But, however different it looks from the 19th century model, it is still called a Poubelle. There's immortality for you!

Like all the other aspects of our culture, garbage collection had become more complex. But, in the end, we all agree on one thing. We just want our garbage to go away. French villages like Aniane have a neat system. There are large, square communal bins on wheels parked in convenient (and inconvenient) spots all around the village. Wherever you live, there is one quite close by. In hill villages, these bins-on-wheels are held precariously by small railings in the street. One might expect vandals to send them careering downhill, but they never do. The French have too much respect for their garbage.

When we had accumulated a respectable amount of garbage, we put it all into one of those the pale blue plastic bags favored by the French. Wine bottles, because of sheer quantity, had to be recycled. We carried the blue sack down the street, tossed it into the to the nearest bin, and our duty was done. Two or three times each week—usually very early in the morning—all the Poubelles were rolled down to the central square with a noise like a several major earthquakes happening at once. They were tipped into a big truck, with more impressive sound effects and away they went, nobody knew where.

We enjoyed this logical, convenient system of communal garbage disposal. But there was something secretive about it. In America, our neighbors can see and note exactly the amount of garbage we produce. Here we got no credit, either for extravagance or economy.

Whenever I set off down the street with the blue bag, I would say: "Just going out to the poubelle." And so I always remembered the jolly, brave Prefect of Paris, who made it all possible. Most of us would like to be remembered for something even half as useful.

9

A Place on the Corner

Living in France made me think about retirement. Why was I paying taxes to support the population of Florida instead of moving to Florida myself? The answer is that, under the American rules, I don't yet qualify for a life of paid leisure.

If I was a French citizen I could retire right now, and take my place among the group of idle men known as "The Senate", who sit all morning on the strategic corner outside the Esplanade Café, then move across the street to play *Pétanque** in the afternoon sun, and then disappear into the bar in the evening. It's not a bad life. Many of these "old boys" are younger than me, and have been retired for years.

A typical French worker can retire at the age of sixty, with seventy percent of his or her former income. Many officials and government employees get to retire even earlier, and on even more generous terms (they are called *"jeunes retraités,"* or young retired people). So a reasonably healthy French man or woman can look forward to a retirement of twenty of thirty years. They call this period of life "The Third Age." It's not even an age of poverty, because pensions are, by tradition, so generous.

Along the Mediterranean coast there are developments of villas and apartments for retirees who come there from all over France and Europe for the food and the climate. With the addition of a few all-you-can-eat salad bars, hip replacement boutiques, and early bird specials, the south of France could compete with Florida in attracting affluent senior citizens.

However, there is the nagging question: who pays? France is in the same demographic vise as every other western country. There are more and more old people, and fewer and fewer young people to support them. Over half the population will be past retiring age by mid-century. This will be tough on the youngsters, who will have to work double shifts to provide comfortable lifestyles for all these elderly folks. The level of taxation doesn't even bear thinking about.

Like anything that touches on social security, this issue is political dynamite. In the local elections nobody wanted to talk about retirement or pensions, let alone taxes. The communist candidate for mayor of Aniane, aged 65, campaigned for the building of a retirement home in the village. The incumbent socialist mayor, aged 52, declared his firm belief in the principle of retirement at 60. None of the other candidates had the courage to disagree.

But the problem of paying for retirement has become so huge that, in 2001, the French employers' organization decided to grasp the nettle. They began talking about changing the system. In particular, they proposed that people should retire later.

You can't help admiring their nerve! The mere mention of later retirement provoked a national wave of outrage. Unions and retirees held angry demonstrations all over France. I briefly joined a protest march of energetic young retired persons in Montpellier. But they were marching too fast for me.

I can't claim to be neutral on this question. It seems entirely good for a society to have a lot of relatively young, relatively affluent retirees. They can participate in education and local politics, do important voluntary work, keep the vast French health service humming, and stand on the corner beside the Esplanade Café. If they were all locked into offices and factories, who would carry out these essential duties?

On the other hand, there's trouble ahead. The proposals for the reform of retirement were stopped dead in their tracks by the wave of protests. The government didn't want to get involved. But unless something changes, young taxpayers will begin to feel the same about retirees as the working citizens of Paris felt about a different kind of aristocracy in 1789. When this taxpayer revolt comes, it could be very nasty indeed. We didn't really expect to see the local teenagers setting up a guillotine in the village square. But we were ready to take the next flight out, to Miami.

Note: "Pétanque" is a version of the game of bowls, peculiar to the South of France. It is usually played on a rough gravel surface, with steel bowls, and almost invariably while smoking cigarettes. Many afficionados swear that it is best played while drunk. Aniane is a big regional center for matches, and sometimes a couple of hundred cars would converge on the bowling ground for all-day matches.

10

A Walk in the Country

The most enthusiastic walkers in Europe are the English and the Germans. They love to hike for miles through the countryside on rough tracks, or no tracks at all, preferably in the middle of a thunderstorm. I blame Martin Luther for this.

The Italians and the French, by contrast, never embraced Luther's bleak view of the human condition. If they can drive, they never walk. In fact, they love their wheels even more passionately than Americans do.

So walking in France is something of a challenge. There is no network of protected footpaths as there is in England. Virtually all property is private and, when the French say **PRIVATE** they mean it. So unless you enjoy confrontations with landowners, who are always angry and often armed, the walking choices are limited.

We like to walk, in moderation. At least once a day we climbed the hill behind Aniane to get a bit of exercise, and to enjoy superb views of the village and the mountains. But the same walk every day got monotonous. We invested in a guide book that promised to show us walks through all the most beautiful scenery in the region, on "safe and well-marked trails."

The walks in the book were divided into four classes: very easy, easy, medium, and difficult. On a good day, we could just about manage the "very easy" category, as long as we rested in bed for the next couple of days. This is mountain country: the scenery is certainly beautiful, as advertised, but it is also very vertical. You don't walk *in* as much as you climb *over* it.

This was not the only hazard of hiking. A linguistic purist might want to argue with the word "safe," when applied to these walks, especially in autumn and winter. The hunting season runs from October through February, and the hills were alive with the sound of gunshots.

The French, or rather French men, do love to shoot things: it scarcely matters what. They kill thirteen million tiny thrushes every year, in a massacre that dismays soft-hearted English bird lovers. But the most coveted prey is the *sanglier*, or wild pig, an ancestor of the wild boars once hunted by French kings. The biggest danger, out there in the countryside, was to be mistaken for a *sanglier*.

Our guide book offered an ominous warning in very small print: "During the hunting season, certain trails were not advised. Consult your local town hall." So we went to our local town hall to ask where it would be safe to walk. The woman at the information desk said: "There are hunters everywhere. They are all looking for wild pigs." She paused and gave me an appraising look. "If I were you," she added, "I would stay at home."

Now I admit that I may look like a wild pig from certain angles. But I do think that hunters, however well-primed with the local wine, should know that that French wild pigs do not speak English, or wear bright check shirts from the Riverhead outlet center. They should pay *some* attention to what they are shooting.

In spite of the hunters, we were determined to enjoy our country walks, and perhaps even move up from the very easy to the easy category, if we survived through the winter. Obviously, we solved the survival problem. We studied photographs of these wild pigs, and noticed that they always go bareheaded, with just little tufts of bristly fur sticking up between their rather large ears. So, just to be on the safe side, Diane bought me a hat.

11

Safety Last

The Monk vulture is the largest vulture in Europe. He gets his name from his stylish tonsure. He's a big bird, with a wingspan of nine feet. When he sits on your lap, you discover that he is also extremely heavy, and has very sharp claws. This is one of the many things I learned by living in France. The educational experience was provided by a bird park near Carcassonne, where we saw a remarkable live show featuring eagles, vultures, hawks, and other predatory birds, all flying free. It was a fully interactive experience. The giant vulture stood on my lap, and an American eagle perched on Diane's head.

The French seem to enjoy a certain amount of risk. Their kamikaze driving style, their smoking habits, their cuisine, and their complicated amours, all help to make their lives more interesting, and shorter. When it comes to entertainment, the French accept hazards that would never be tolerated in America. The display in the bird park, for example, was a whole series of accidents scarcely even waiting to happen. Big, fierce birds with razor-sharp beaks and claws were zooming around the heads of the paying customers, landing impartially on adults and children. The scratches I got from the vulture's claws would be worth at least a million dollars in damages in America, quite apart from any interesting diseases that I might have picked up.

A popular local walk from the village of St. Guilhem went straight up the side of a mountain. It was not so much a walk as a climb, over jagged, slippery rocks, with sheer drops on one side, and sometimes on both. At one point, the path skirted a precipice almost a thousand feet high. There were no railings or warning signs. Yet, on a summer Sunday, the narrow path was crowded with families, including small children, all wearing highly unsuitable shoes, most of them smoking, and accompanied by tiny dogs, scrambling happily upwards as if this was as safe as Main Street in Disneyland.

France is notably short of warning signs and safety rules. Nobody tells you, for example, that you shouldn't put plastic bags over your head. When a school bus stops the other traffic goes roaring past at full speed, and the kids have to jump. You must learn to watch out for yourself. When you fill a prescription at the pharmacy, not only does your medication come in a container that can be opened without a PhD in engineering and a tool kit, but also the pills are not counted. It is assumed that the patient will pay attention to the doctor's instructions, and stop when the course of treatment is over—even if there are dozens of pills left.

Many of the sidewalks in Aniane were positively dangerous. Old tree roots had broken through and created jagged pyramids of broken concrete. There were holes big enough to put your leg through. At one point, just outside a busy newspaper stand, the sidewalk simply stopped, and there was a three-foot drop. This was easy to miss in broad daylight, and totally invisible at night. But nobody cared because it had been that way for at least a century, which made it OK. Road works and building works generally weren't fenced off. Pedestrians just climbed over and through them to reach their destinations.

The elderly folks of the village were surprisingly spry and active. I never saw a wheelchair or a Zimmer frame. It is tempting to attribute their health to the fact that they have been clambering over obstacles in the street all their lives. Alternatively, of course, it may be a form of Darwinian selection—the survival of the fittest.

This casual attitudes to danger in public places could be a reaction against the suffocating embrace of the welfare state, which provides cradle to grave security. But it's more plausibly explained by the fact that personal injury lawsuits are relatively rare in France, and judges are unsympathetic. You can't expect to be compensated for carelessness or risky behavior, or even for stupidity. It's nice to be treated as an adult, when your own safety is concerned.

The villagers had their share of accidents and misfortunes, but they seemed to live easily with the fact that bad things happen to good people. "That's how life is," they said. "You never know what's going to fall on your head."

But this sensible fatalism may soon be a thing of the past. When we rented a new French-made car we found that we had acquired a mechanical nursemaid. "Your right hand door is open," she scolded. "The temperature is zero degrees, beware of black ice." "You have exceeded the maximum legal speed limit," and so on. This car, nicknamed Eloise, had a whole repertoire of unwanted warnings and advice. I was half expecting her to remind me to get my hair cut, or to put less garlic in the fish sauce.

Another straw in the wind was a creeping ban on smoking in public places. The French are the biggest smokers in Europe—42% men and 27% women light up, and 60,000 lay down their lives for tobacco every year. Generally speaking, smoking was tolerated everywhere. The village postman went on his rounds in a haze of smoke from his *Gauloise*, within a larger haze of blue smoke from his Vélo. "No Smoking" signs were a joke, or a gesture to the paranoia of American tourists. We rode a steam railway in the Cévennes that had *défense de fumer* signs displayed everywhere. But the carriages were completely open and every time the train plunged into a tunnel everyone was engulfed in choking smoke, through which the "No Smoking" signs could be dimly seen.

But sometimes "No Smoking" signs were serious. Lyon Airport was one such place, and the entire concourse was filled with nervous, twitching, angry people. A ban on smoking in France is like a ban on breathing: it drives people crazy. But it suggests that health food stores, and warning notices on giant vultures and plastic bags cannot be far behind.

12

Games of Chance

The French have always been ready to take a gamble. It was a long shot in 1789 when the citizens of Paris took on the absolute monarch Louis XVI, and won the jackpot. At other times, for example in 1415 at the Battle of Agincourt (the one with Laurence Olivier), and in 1815 at Waterloo, their luck was out. But that's the nature of gambling—you win some, and you lose most.

The French love gambling in all its forms. The village newspaper shops carried a dozen papers devoted entirely to horse racing. Aniane also had a bar that doubled as an O.T.B. Their slogan was *"Jouer avec les emotions"* (play with your emotions). You could place your bets right there, and watch your horse limp sluggishly past the post on a giant TV screen, while you inhaled industrial-strength tobacco smoke, and swallowed a much-needed drink. It was an efficient if not an economical way to enjoy several vices at once.

For those who didn't choose to hang out in bars, the favorite form of gambling in Aniane was Loto, which is a kind of bingo. Everyone ran a Loto game as a form of fundraising: firefighters, senior citizens, sports clubs, schools, and of course the churches. The local Communist Party ran its own Loto game at Christmas. They were rather embarrassed about it, being both atheists and anti-capitalists. But they admitted that they needed the money.

For the players Loto was not really about money. It was about community, and fun, and above all about food. The payoff was more gastronomic than financial. The players gathered round a table in the firehouse or the community hall, and it was heads down for the big prizes.

Prize list for a Loto game in Aniane: eight hams; eight turkeys; five pork loins; six sheep quarters, two half pigs, eight baskets of poultry, and one surprise.

Perhaps the "Surprise" was something for vegetarians. But I doubt it.

Certain questions came to mind, especially about the two half-pigs. For example: which half? One can imagine several ways of dividing a pig. If you win half a pig, where do you put it? And what if you happen to be Jewish?

I wanted to try my luck in one of these local Loto games, but there was a serious language barrier. I slipped into the community hall one day when a game was in progress. The caller was delivering numbers at such machine-gun speed in such a picturesque local accent that I couldn't understand a single word. I might have won a whole ménagerie, and been none the wiser.

If your dream is to be a millionaire, rather than just to have a very full refrigerator, there is a French national lottery on the American model. The lottery had its 25th anniversary in 2000, and is the most popular game of chance in France: 38% of French population plays, and 7,500 new (franc) millionaires have been created.

But the French have gone one better. In addition to the regular weekly lottery, they have invented the Rapido lottery. This also takes place in the bar. Rapido lives up to its name. You choose eight numbers, pay the barman about a dollar, and wait for the draw. You don't have to wait long. Rapido is drawn every five minutes, day and night, and the numbers appear on a screen right there above the bar. If you lose, as I invariably did, the next draw is only five minutes away.

It was irresistible, it was hypnotic, and frankly it is shameful for the French state to encourage this kind of addictive gambling for the weak-willed and feeble-minded inhabitants of small villages, where there are very few other forms of entertainment. What's worse, it made it almost impossible for some of us to finish our French homework.

13

The Circus Comes to Town

In France the circus is an art form. There are a hundred and twenty special schools for circus performers, and more than two hundred traveling circuses. At its best, a French circus is the ultimate live entertainment. But, like French wines, they vary a lot. Not all of them are genuinely French, and some should not be consumed under any circumstances.

When I was growing up in England the circus came to our neighborhood twice a year. These were the two high points of my personal calendar. When the circus came to Aniane, in spite of my misgivings about performing animals, I couldn't resist. The circus, being a wordless entertainment, is perfect for foreigners and for the generations that have grown up within the claustrophobic limits of the small video screen, a live spectacle like the circus must surely be enormously exciting. The circus is interactive, three-dimensional, and it has both surround sound and surround smells. This had to be better than any video entertainment.

The whole village was plastered with posters, showing clowns, lions and elephants. On the appointed day a rather small red and yellow tent appeared on the sports ground. Exotic animals were seen grazing beside the football field, driving the local dogs mad with excitement and curiosity. I was in much the same state myself, until I got inside the tent.

The largest circuses on the road create a convoy of trucks more than a mile long. Cirque Zavata, which came from Spain, had three trucks, and the tent was as small inside as it was outside. The actual ring about twenty feet across, half the standard size. The most expensive ringside seats were six dirty plastic lawn chairs. The cheap seats were hard and very dirty wooden benches. In spite of the plain accomodations the "usherette" demanded a tip so aggressively that even the French customers were shocked. This did not look promising. But the kids of the village and their parents crammed enthusiastically into the small space. We were embarrassed to be there without a child, although Diane said that my presence made this unnecessary.

The show did not begin with the traditional grand parade of performers, for reasons that soon became obvious. A small pony ran round and round the small ring, while a stout young man in a blue jacket cracked a whip. A slightly smaller pony came in, and did the same. Then a very small pony indeed, about the size of a goat, came in and ran round and round. I was getting dizzy.

As one act followed another, it became clear that they had started with their best shot. Everything else was worse. A mangy camel and a depressed llama walked round and round the ring. The ringmaster reappeared, with a different coat, in the guise of a juggler. We know a distinguished scientists who is a better juggler than this clown who, at one point, dropped all his flaming torches and nearly set fire to the tent. This would have been very bad news, because the safety exits were tied firmly shut.

We were afraid that this untalented juggler would reappear as an equally incompetent lion tamer. But the lions featured on the circus posters proved to be two performing domestic cats. It soon became clear that the repertoire was limited not only by the skills of the performers, but also by the fact that there were very few of them. They just kept changing clothes. The ticket sellers and usherettes appeared in the ring, incongruously dressed in sequins and heavy work boots. The unsteady acrobats were the same as the un-funny clowns, who were the same as the guys who worked the spotlights and sold the popcorn. We speculated that the camel was a llama in disguise, and soon figured out that the total ensemble consisted of six adults, eight animals, and three young children.

The so-called animal acts were as bad as I had feared. But I wasn't prepared for the children. They had obviously been conditioned and trained on a very short leash, just like the animals. Especially pathetic was a tiny, fragile looking six-year-old girl acrobat, who was tossed around dangerously by her trainer. Then she performed a long routine with metal hoops, all alone, until she was flat out exhausted.

The children in the audience sensed that something was wrong. They looked away, and became more interested in each other than in the performance. I was totally disgusted by this tawdry spectacle. It used to be every child's dream, including mine, to run away to join the circus. I used to wonder sometimes about children who were actually born into the circus, and feel sorry for them because they had nothing to run away *to*. But these young performers must surely dream of running away *from* the circus. When they do, I hope they take the wretched animals with them.

14

Nothing is Easy

Winter in the south of France was not the way we imagined it, and probably not the way you imagine it. We watched the evening weather forecast on TV with as much attention as New Englanders, and storm clouds came marching across the screen with tedious regularity. French weather forecasts are more stylish than ours, but the end result is much the same: it rains a lot. On winter mornings the village was usually wet, dark, deserted, and almost sinister.

There were many winds, with poetic names. The Tramontane from the northwest gave way to the Mistral from the north, then the Marin from the south. Sometimes they all blew at once. People didn't pay attention to the poetic names: they just huddled indoors.

The odd thing was that nobody seemed prepared for this. They seemed to imagine that they were living in the mythical south of France where starlets at the Cannes film festival are always disrobing on golden beaches under a blazing sun. Even villagers whose families had been there for generations hadn't quite come to terms with the fact that they had a winter—every year.

Many of the older village houses didn't have heating. It wasn't that the owners couldn't afford it, but they seemed to feel that they *shouldn't* need heating, down there by the Mediterranean, and therefore it would be an extravagance. When invited out to dinner, we soon learned to dress in layers.

We were fortunate to have a kind of heating system in our house—an oil stove, strategically situated between the kitchen and the living room. It was more than just a stove: it was a whole home entertainment system.

In America our heating system was invisible and inaudible. It whispered into action when the thermostat fell below comfort level. So we found this oil stove a bit daunting at first. Starting the thing up was only slightly less complicated than launching the space shuttle. It began down in the wine cellar, where the oil tank was lurking. We checked the oil level with a long stick. Then we switched on the pump, which made a noise like a very old food processor, whipped the lid off the stove, and shone a flashlight into its stygian depths. A black trickle of oil might eventually appear, dragged up from the basement by the pump. One of us would hold the flashlight while the other would throw lighted matches at the oil until it caught fire. This usually took six or seven matches. Then we clapped the lid before being overcome by the fumes, and waited until a fierce smoky flame appeared. This was the signal to turn the main control up. Then we had heat. Things could and did go wrong at every stage of this procedure, and other things could affect the outcome—for example if the chimney was cold, or the Mistral was blowing hard, or our horoscopes predicted a bad day.

From time to time the oil ran out. Then we had to call the oil deliveryman. In Long Island or Connecticut, oil companies phone almost every day, with tempting special offers. They deliver oil on a regular schedule, so that you never run out. In Aniane, getting oil was more of a challenge. The street was narrow, so we needed an oil deliveryman with either a very long hose, or a very thin truck. There was only one, and his whereabouts and his movements were an impenetrable mystery. It took weeks to persuade our neighbors to disclose his secret phone number, and he refused to say when or whether he might actually deliver our oil. One of us had to wait in the house all day, every day. At last he came dragging his long hose, and sloshed a few hundred liters of dark, smelly stuff into the tank. He wanted to be paid in cash, of course. Everyone in France demands cash. I just don't know how they keep track of it all, when the time comes to pay their taxes.

Just before we left Aniane we learned that natural gas was coming to the village: clean, economical heat, always on line. They were digging trenches and installing meters along all the streets. I hope that the oil deliveryman is re-thinking his business strategy right now.

15

Spoilt for Choice

On December 20 there weren't many signs of Christmas in Aniane. The town hall had been decorated with a few colored lights, and Madame Lilli had put cards and a few seasonal objects in the window of her boutique. But that was about it. No houses were visibly decorated, no stores were playing Christmas carols over loudspeakers. In this, as in other things, the inhabitants of Aniane seemed disinclined to go over the top.

After the hysterical intensity of the holiday season in America, this relaxed attitude was something of a relief. But it did make us rather nervous. It was like driving with someone going at a hundred miles an hour, with just one finger on the steering wheel. After all, The holidays *were* coming. They could not be stopped. Preparations had to be made, vast amounts of money had to be spent very quickly, credit cards had to be run up to the limit. Yet here were these French people, on December 20, strolling around, chatting and casually shopping for bread and onions, as if they didn't have a care in the world. In the nearby city of Montpellier the first Christmas decorations had appeared on December 15, allowing a generous ten days for holiday madness. On Long Island you're not surprised to see them in August.

My theory is that this is because of the French Revolution. In 1792 the revolutionaries, hoping to erase memories of the old regime, introduced an entirely new calendar, with new names for the months and new festivals. Christmas was *not* included, and Christmas shopping was therefore eliminated. I don't think the French have ever forgotten what a glorious relief this was. Ever since Christmas is restored to their calendar by Napoleon in 1806, they have been rather half-hearted about it.

Christmas shopping in Aniane was not easy. The small stores in the village didn't offer much in the way of gifts, unless you wanted to give bread, meat, or vegetables. Shopping in the city would be an admission of defeat. The closest thing we had to a general store was Monsieur Vidal's strange establishment, hidden at the end of a blind alley. Whatever you might want, Monsieur Vidal was likely to have at least one: one 60 watt light bulb, one ironing board, one straw Panama hat, one packet of floppy disks, and so on. If, by an unlucky chance, an earlier customer had bought the particular item you needed he would go out at lunchtime in his old Peugeot and buy it for you at the supermarket in the next town. That's service. It was also ecologically friendly. One car trip by Monsieur Vidal saved a dozen trips by his customers.

Naturally, his selection was limited. What you saw was what you got. There was no point in fussing over color or style, or even condition. I almost bought his one Panama hat, in spite of the fact that it had obviously been on the shelf beside the rabbit food for years, was covered with a thick layer of dust, and was several sizes too big.

In principle I love this kind of retail establishment. When I shopped with Monsieur Vidal I escaped from the tyranny of choice. Too much choice makes me dizzy. But, at this time of year, with a list of gifts to buy, I had to admit that no choice at all was not enough. Monsieur Vidal had apparently added nothing to his stock for the holiday season, except one incongruous plastic beach ball. There were a few dusty ornaments, and some old toys in faded cardboard boxes. But essentially all the same stuff was in the same places, with the cat sleeping undisturbed on a heap of shoeboxes. With the best will in the world, it was hard to get into the holiday shopping mood there. The consumerist impulse died when confronted with Monsieur Vidal's stock.

There was only one solution: everyone on our list, including children and teetotalers, would get a bottle of wine this year. After all, we were in France, which produces thirty thousand different wines. Aniane alone had six vineyards offering two-dozen varieties, from the suspiciously cheap to the most outrageously expensive. When it came to Holiday shopping, we were positively spoilt for choice.

16

Living in the Past

Spring is carnival time in France. Every town and village has to have one. These events are rooted in local history, which means that no two carnivals are quite the same. They do have things in common, of course. You can't have a carnival without a Carnival Queen, and a parade of floats through the streets. You can't have any kind of carnival without music, and costumes, and amusements, and cotton candy. "It's for the children," everyone said. But I had the distinct impression that the children would be just as happy to stay at home with their video games. Carnival is about history and memory, which means that it's really for the grownups.

The Languedoc is particularly rich in carnival traditions. Just own the road, in Gignac, they have the festival of the donkey, which commemorates an event in the eighth century—more than 1,200 years ago. These people have long memories. On that distant date, the good people of Gignac were saved from a Saracen attack by the braying of their donkeys. It's not clear what the Saracens were doing in Gignac, so far from home base. Perhaps they were indulging in a bit of tourism, or simply lost. But, regardless of logic or probability, a symbolic donkey made of wood and cloth is paraded through the streets during the annual carnival. Many other villages have an historic animal symbol that appears in their carnival—a bull in Mèze, for reasons we won't discuss, a wolf (appropriately enough) at Loupian, a foal at Pézenas, and a black pig at St. André de Sagonis—each one with a story attached.

The village of Aniane strikes a rather odd note in this parade of allegorical animals. At carnival time, when darkness falls, the citizens themselves parade through the streets, carrying candles and wearing long white robes, rather like nightdresses. This was an event worth waiting for and, of course, it also recalled some ancient history—although in this case it went back a mere eight hundred years. In the twelfth century, this area was settled by a bunch of heretics called the Cathars. They lived very simply, fasting frequently, denying themselves all sensual pleasures, and mortifying their bodies with various discomforts such as a complete lack of central heating. They also believed in two gods, one good and one bad. This was considered by the Pope to be very wicked, especially as they identified him with the dark side. He launched a crusade against them in 1209, and the Cathars and their descendants were persecuted for the next five hundred years. The repression ended only with the Edict of Tolerance in 1787, just before the French Revolution made the whole thing irrelevant.

To make a very long story short, the medieval costume drama in Aniane commemorates the heroic resistance of the Cathars during all those years. The long white robes were intended as a kind of disguise, although it's hard to imagine anything more conspicuous.

Perhaps as a result of their resistance, this region at the southern tip of the Cévennes has remained by far the least Catholic part of France. The protestant Huguenots found refuge here for centuries, and this legacy of religious non-conformism lives on. It's a paradox, really. The south of France has the image of being a laid-back paradise of self-indulgence. But the cyclists give the game away.

Every weekend, winter and summer, the mountain roads were full of bicycles, even though almost every French family owns a car. These cyclists inherit and incarnate eight hundred years of the puritan tradition—first the Cathars, and then the Protestants. They know in their hearts that we were not put on this earth to have a good time, but rather to strive and to suffer. They ride dozens of miles over dangerous mountain roads, in all weathers, wearing very silly costumes. They pedal up inclines that reduce cars to bottom gear, their faces contorted with the effort. They ignore the suicidal traffic whizzing past a couple of inches away. In general, it's clear that they are having an absolutely horrible time.

One of our friends lived in a village forty kilometers away, over a mountain. She was a woman of mature age who owned a perfectly good car. This did not stop her from cycling two or three hours over the mountain to visit us, often carrying a load of olives or wine on her racing bicycle.

"It's good for my health," she would say, dripping sweat on to our doorstep and looking like the last survivor of a marathon across the Sahara desert.

In this improbable way the misery caused by all those hundreds of years of religious warfare is remembered and reproduced on the roads of France every day. The Cathars in their long white robes may be a thing of the past but, thanks to these noble cyclists, Puritanism Lives!

17

The Village Community

The people of Aniane, as we soon discovered, were bound together by more than physical closeness. They had a strong common identity as "Anianais," just as the people in the next village saw themselves as "Ginacois." This feeling of community was constantly reinforced by common activities. Although the village had only 1,500 inhabitants and you could walk across it in five minutes, there was always something going on—free concerts, poetry readings, pétanque matches—something for everybody. It was all orchestrated from the eighteenth century town hall right in the center of the village where the mayor presided more like a tribal leader than a politician.

Public spaces were intensively used—the sports field was claimed by the circus, and for outdoor concerts. The Place des Penitents in the center of the village hosted flea markets, fish stalls, outdoor dinners, brass bands and art shows. The Post Office car park was taken over for a motorcycle show, a country fair, a midsummer celebration, and more music. The theater in the old monastery put on regular plays, some of them classics, and the village hall was the venue for Loto, agricultural events, and live pop music concerts. The twelfth century Chapel of the Penitents had a new art show every month, and the Catholic church of Saint Sauveur hosted some splendid classical music concerts. We might almost have been in a big city rather than in a very small village. The community activities wore us out.

There were a surprising number of formal and informal groups. Old men who hung out at the Esplanade café, young people who hung out at the opposite end of the village, in the PMU bar, several political parties, the wine growers' association, the Club of the Third Age, a theater group, and an organization called *Vivre à Aniane*. The latter was made up of middle-aged people, ironically known as *soixante huitards* (sixty eighters)—referring to the wave of youth revolts in France in 1968 that receded and left these fiftysomethings beached in places like Aniane. They worked against the odds to bring more liberal and modern attitudes to the village.

Public benches were everywhere. The *banc publique* is a French institution, and the popular singer George Brassens wrote a famous love song about it. People actually used these benches, not so much for romantic encounters as for gossiping and quiet sitting. This is not a negligible part of village public life. You'd have to walk a long way in most American towns to find a public bench. The idea that a fit and healthy person might want to just stop and sit for a while is alien to us.

Halloween, which happened just two months after we arrived, is a good illustration of how a strong community deals with a new challenge. The French, for some bizarre reason, have begun to adopt this quintessentially American death festival. In Aniane, it was celebrated for the very first time during our stay. But the Anianais did it their way. An announcement was sent around to every house, and reinforced by the village DJ. If you wanted to give out candy (or *petites friandises*) to the children on October 31st, you first had to register at the town hall. Registrants received a free Halloween orange balloon to be displayed outside the door on Halloween night. Children (with parents or teachers, not alone) were allowed to call at houses marked with balloons, only between 6 p.m. and 8 p.m. All other visits were forbidden.

These precautions reflected the general view of Halloween in America as an orgy of teenage vandalism. The teenagers of Aniane were firmly told that this was something for little kids, so naturally they scorned it. The rules also protected old or sick (or just plain misanthropic) villagers from being disturbed by unwanted visitors.

This highly controlled version of Halloween was a great success. The evening was magical, with troupes of excited tots in costume hurrying from one marked door to the next, and the gendarme patrolling sedately behind them. There was no vandalism, and no noise. However, the village was divided about whether to have Halloween again next year. Some people saw it as the thin end of a monstrous web of disorder and chaos, and others denounced it as a reversion to paganism. But can any society on earth resist the commercial juggernaut of American culture for very long?

On the feast of Saint Jean on June 23, the whole village turned out to *sauter le feu* (jump over the fire) in the main car park. The local firefighters created a blaze out of bracken and old vine stems and, starting with the youngest, everyone jumped over it. This ceremony results in a number of minor burns every year, but this is all part of the fun. Saint Jean is patron saint of priests, who suffered when the devil allegedly set fire to his bed. But, although nobody was willing to admit it, jumping the fire is clearly a remnant of some pagan midsummer celebration.

A great deal of this lively community life remained obscure to us because of language problems and a natural reluctance on the part of the villagers to explain themselves to nosy outsiders. We never figured out the mystery of the cats and the water bottles, described above, which might also be the shadow of some ancient magic ritual. About six months into our stay we removed the bottles, attracting disapproving looks and headshakes from the neighbors. Nothing happened.

Part II

Language Problems

18

French as He is Spoke

When we came to live in France Diane already spoke good French, and I could stumble along in a simple conversation. I assumed that it would be only a matter of weeks before I was speaking the language, if not with Gallic fluency then at least with some degree of competence. I expected to learn effortlessly by osmosis and total immersion.

This miracle failed to happen. Simple negotiations in the post office or the grocery store regularly turned into hilarious comedies of misunderstanding. I was entertaining more people in Aniane than I ever did in my short career as a humorist. Shopkeepers smiled when they saw me coming, anticipating a few minutes of harmless hilarity at the Englishman's expense. I was quickly becoming a local "character."

So I decided to take a class.

I've never been good at languages because languages are mostly about arbitrary rules, and I hate arbitrary rules. French has more arbitrary and more bizarre rules than any other language. There is a whole national institution, the French Academy, dedicated to inventing and defending these rules, so that no foreigner ever has a chance to get them right. Gender, for example: you probably remember from school that every French noun is either masculine or feminine, except for a few that swing both ways. Since the language has thousands of nouns, this means a lot of guesswork, and it is very, very hard to make a good guess. For example France, the country, is feminine *(la France)*, while French, the language, is masculine *(le français)*. How is anybody supposed to guess that? The answer, of course, is that you are *not* supposed to guess it. You are supposed to get it wrong and reveal yourself as an utterly ignorant and stupid foreigner. David Sedaris, in one of his entertaining dispatches from Paris on National Public Radio, confessed that he bought two of everything so as to use the plural form and avoid the trap of guessing the right gender. I often used this trick myself. It works fine, as long as the object of your desire isn't obstinately singular, like a haircut or heart transplant (both, by the way, feminine). The limitations of my French trapped me in a formless, genderless, present tense. I desperately wanted to change this.

Language incompetence has a bad effect on one's self-image. A person who can't talk properly is immediately reduced to childishness. Even my elegant French teacher was a study in perplexity when she tried and failed to speak English. And while French accented English may sound sexy, English accented French most definitely does not! That's why kids brought up in the American style hate languages. Learning a language is one long exercise in humiliation. Having a French name (Bouchier) made things worse. Everyone *expected* me to speak French, just as you would expect someone called Smith to speak English. But my last French ancestor left for England in 1810, and nobody in our family has spoken a word of French since.

I enrolled in a language class in the heart of the handsome city of Montpellier. There were many schools to choose from and, lacking any other criterion, I chose the one on Rue August Comte. Comte was the inventor of sociology and the father of positivism. He was quite mad, but I've always admired him. He was born in Montpellier almost exactly two centuries ago, and his name on the street seemed like a good omen.

I took a placement test. I came fully prepared with all the usual test phrases: "Can I look it up in the dictionary?" "My pencil is broken." "I have to go to the bathroom." None of this did any good. The teacher snatched the test paper away before I was finished, and struck out most of my answers muttering "*incroyable,*" and "*extraordinaire.*" We tried some conversation.

"You're very clever at making up sentences without genders or verbs," she said (actually I think "cunning" was the term she used).

"How long have you been learning French?" she demanded.

"About fifty years," I replied truthfully,

Fifty years was obviously not enough. My linguistic self-esteem, never very robust, was completely shattered. I expected to be assigned to the lowest class of *débutants*, or absolute beginners. But I must have caught Madame Patricia on a particularly good day. Or perhaps she was looking for a challenge. She wrote on my folder "Intermediate Class."

"The *lowest level* of the Intermediate Class." she added, before I could get too pleased with myself.

Thus I entered the quaintly-named category of *faux débutants*, or beginners who pretend to know something.

The following week I began my daily commute of about forty minutes into Montpellier, over hills and through vineyards, to be in class at nine o'clock. Three intensive hours every morning was considered the minimum dose of French necessary to cure someone at my level.

I was the oldest member of the class by about thirty-five years. At first I felt like a kind of grandfather figure, but then I realized that there were worse things than spending three hours every day in the company of a dozen (mostly) charming and (mostly) very pretty young women from all over the world. One of the few male students was an Arab from Oman, who was looking for a second wife. Nobody volunteered.

The group changed week by week. At various times it included English, Americans, Japanese and Germans, some Scandinavians, Africans, and Italians, an Egyptian model, a glamorous Polish singer, an agricultural engineer from the Sultanate of Oman, an Icelandic girl like a tiny blonde elf, a Spanish policeman, an albino doctor from Syria, a super-elegant Swiss lady who always looked above it all, and a Brazilian bombshell who made it very difficult for any of us males to concentrate on our verbs.

We had conversation periods every morning, on topics carefully chosen to avoid politics, religion, and anything else that might give offence to all the different sensibilities packed into that small room. This didn't leave us much to talk about. But we talked nevertheless, and our conversations were like a surrealistic collaboration between Lewis Carroll, Samuel Becket and Marcel Marceau. The high point for me was when a Danish student called Ken and I presented the bewildered class with the whole of Monty Python's Dead Parrot sketch, in fractured French. (If you have no idea what this means in any language, don't worry about it).

It was interesting to get a perspective on the young people from different countries. They lived up to their stereotypes: the Germans were serious and intent on learning 'the rules'; the Italians and Spanish were relaxed and insouciant; the Scandinavians were cheerful and sensible; the Japanese were totally paranoid; the Americans were undisciplined and lazy; and the British were confused and apologetic.

After three months, I left my French class for the last time. I'd like to pretend that this departure marked my achievement of perfect comprehension and fluency. But the truth is that I had learned enough to understand how far I had to go.

I expected to finish the class with relief. For three months I'd commuted into Montpellier every day during the morning rush hour, and sat for a total of two hundred hours, in a state of complete confusion, in a cold room, on a very hard chair, with a bunch of people who could have been my grandchildren.

But it was a wrench to leave those people. We were a miniature United Nations—united by our tenuous grasp of the French language

Every day, one of us had to present a short speech to the whole class, in French. We played silly games with words, we laughed a lot. Above all we endured the hard slog of grammar. I cannot imagine why the French need *fourteen* tenses of verbs, when we get along fine in English with only seven. In addition to all this, we got homework every day—a short essay and a grammar exercise. It was virtually a full-time job.

I learned, among other things, that younger brains really do move faster. It's chastening to discover that, when it comes to remembering grammar and vocabulary, age and experience count for less than nothing.

It was pleasing to see how the whole class took on some of the nicest French habits, such as daily hugs and kisses all around. I've never seen this happen in a British or American college class. I missed seeing these charming, intelligent young people every day. They included me very cheerfully into their company, even though I must have seemed like a peculiarly inarticulate grandfather.

Above all, I missed my teacher. I'd forgotten what a pleasure it is to have a gifted teacher. Madame Patricia was stylish, charming, professional, endlessly patient, and strict. Her strictness was important. I was often tempted to stay in bed, especially when some particularly nasty grammar was on the program or it was my turn to give a talk to the class. Madame Patricia did not tolerate this kind of backsliding. Once she demoted me to the lower class for a week, because I had failed to come to grips with the subjunctive.

"It is necessary to come to class every day, David," she would admonish me.

Nor did she tolerate my feeble attempts at humor in the French language.

"It is necessary sometimes to be serious, David." she said, many times. I did my best.

Madame Patricia was a most interesting woman. She was born in Syria, and was quite beautiful. Diane seemed to think that I shouldn't have lunch with her on my own, even though this would have been a good chance to improve my French at little extra cost. I'm sure that this restriction slowed my progress in irregular verbs.

If I know any French at all today it's thanks to those two hundred hours of gentle torture in Madame Patricia's class. On my last day I took a farewell picture of them all. That picture really is worth a thousand words.

19

Hors de Combat

My French classes may have not done much to improve my French, but they have made me *au courant* with an alarming *malaise* in our own culture. The French are taking over the English language—probably as a prelude to some greater act of *lese-majesté* such as revoking the Louisiana Purchase, reclaiming Canada, or reversing the result of the Napoleonic Wars.

When I started a *dossier* on this phenomenon, with the intention of publishing an *exposé,* I uncovered an *embarras de richesses*. The French invasion of our language began with the Norman invasion of England in 1066, and (*plus ça change, plus c'est la même chose*) it continues today, under cover of a clever *mascarade*. We were constantly told that the French language was being destroyed by a *mélange* of English words. It's something of a *cause célèbre* there that Franglais *clichés* like "le weekend" and "le snack bar" are polluting their precious vocabulary. My *riposte* is that, *au contraire*, it is the English language that is being polluted. French words have been imported *en masse*. French is very much *à la mode* in the *avant garde* world of *belles lettres*. But it takes *finesse* to walk the line between genuine *savoir faire* and the false *panache* of a mere *poseur.*

You see what I mean. As we say *au revoir* to the *fin de siècle,* we scarcely know which language we are speaking any more.

If you are something of a *bon vivant,* you know that French had long been the language of *haute cuisine*. We go to the *bistro* for *hors d'oeuvres* and an *entrée, à la carte,* wish one another *bon appetit,* and wonder whether the *plat du jour* of chicken *à la* king would be more *piquant* with a *soupçon* of *bouquet garni*. But food is only the tip of the iceberg. The French have pulled off a *tour de force* of verbal imperialism, claiming *carte blanche* to rewrite the entire English language, and I don't see any chance of a *rapprochement* unless we isolate the whole French nation behind a linguistic *cordon sanitaire*.

As a writer, I can't afford to be *blasé* about this. My native tongue is *en route* to becoming a *pastiche*, or even a *purée*. Sometimes, *faute de mieux*, I find myself using a French word, because it happens to be the *mot juste*. But consider this: if an English-speaking person is looking for a job, he or she must send out a short account of their work experience—not an old-fashioned Latin *curriculum vitae* but a subversive French *résumé*. In today's *laissez-faire* economy, where *nouveau riche entrepreneurs* are too *blasé* to read a whole life history, it might be more *à propos* for candidates to send a *précis* of their *résumé*, or even a simple *aide-mémoire*.

My *cri du coeur* went unheeded by the *Chargé d'Affaires* at the British consulate, who dismissed my concerns as *outré*. I discussed the problem, *tête à tête*, with my *petite* French teacher. She was a *connaisseuse* of language, and I thought we had a good *rapport*. But it was *déjà vu* all over again. She was quite *brusque,* and we soon reached an *impasse*. "This is some stupid *bête noire* of the English," she said." It's completely *passé*. It is never *comme il faut* to use French words in English."

If there is any good news in this sad history it is that I'll soon be able to speak French perfectly, simply by speaking English. So my *raison d'être* for learning this *soi-disant* foreign language is rapidly disappearing, and may soon receive the *coup de grace*. The triumph of French over English is virtually a *fait accompli*.

Part III

Travels with a Citroen

20

Survival of the Fastest

Our transportation in France was a lively little Citroen Xsara in a striking shade of electric blue. She carried us safely over many thousands of kilometers, and we were often grateful for her punchy brakes and her balletic ability to swerve out of trouble without ever losing her grip on the road.

The transition from American to European driving is always a shock. Your European car seems the size of a skateboard, you are surrounded by gigantic trucks, and everybody is hurtling along at 80 m.p.h. The French are not aggressive drivers, but they are *competitive*. They want to see what you can do, what you can *survive*, in much the same spirit as the other drivers in a demolition derby. For the first couple of hours after I arrive in France I always find myself gripping the wheel tightly, sweating with anxiety, and trying to decide which of the major world religions offers the best deal in the case of sudden death. But, as the kilometers roll by I relax into the universal religion of French motorists: fatalism.

Fatalism is built into the French highway system. Among the great scenic treasures of this lovely nation are the millions of stately plane trees that line so many of her highways. They were planted two centuries ago to provide shade for Napoleon's marching armies. But they are not exactly a safety feature for modern drivers: one mistake, and you're dead. The most famous victim was Albert Camus, who met his fatal tree near Sens in 1960. In 2001, to reduce the numbers of casualties, the government introduced a scheme to remove or replant five million plane trees by 2006. The landscape will be destroyed but motorists, like cats with nine lives, will have more chances to survive their own suicidal driving habits.

My reaction to this scheme is that trees don't kill people, crazy drivers kill people. The French love to drive too fast. I'm not a particularly slow or nervous driver myself, but I can't keep up with them unless I have put my personal affairs in order, and achieved the right philosophical state of mind.

Speeding isn't limited to the highways. The narrow, crowded towns and villages are a challenge for this nation of creative drivers. When a French motorist sees traffic backing up ahead, he doesn't necessarily slow down or stop. He (or she) just throws the car into reverse, and keeps moving. So it's important to remember that, just because you are looking at the *rear* end of a car, it doesn't mean that it's not heading *towards* you at full speed. And if you think "pedestrian precinct" indicates a safe haven, you'd better check your life insurance

The statistics speak for themselves. France easily surpasses the rest of Europe in vehicular mayhem, with half a million dead since 1950. That's twice as many fatal accidents per head as Britain, and more even than Germany or Italy, if you can imagine it. The United States is not even in the competition. This is not the fault of the French highways, which are excellent, but of the motorists, who are not. Speed limits may be as low as twenty miles per hour in town, and as high as eighty on the open road. These numbers are completely irrelevant. The only real limits are imposed by the power of the cars and the blind optimism of their drivers.

On my morning commute into Montpellier I stayed within the safe region of eighty to ninety miles an hour, because I didn't want to test out my language skills on the French police. That is still an awful lot faster than you can travel on the Long Island Expressway or I-95 in rush hours. Nevertheless, I was passed without effort or apology by just about every other vehicle on the road, except for a few heavy trucks and very small cars driven by very old ladies. In a recent survey, 91% of all vehicles were clocked above the maximum limit of 130 k.p.h. (80 m.p.h.) on major highways.

Here's a small observation on road safety in France. We stopped for lunch at the Brasserie de la Gare in a small town called Gonfil. The bar was full of truck drivers, taking their lunch break. They stayed in the bar drinking glass after glass of the strong liquor called Pastis for about an hour, while we had lunch in the dining room. Then they all came into the dining room and started their lunch, which lasted another hour. During that time, we watched a table of six drivers absorb five one-liter carafes of red wine. Then they climbed into their big trucks and drove away. Every road trip you survive in France is a small victory over fate and culture.

The Gendarmes claim that speed is the main cause of accidents, but they don't seem keen to do much about it. A law passed in 2001 required the automatic confiscation of the license of anybody caught driving more than twenty-five miles per hour over the limit. But I never saw a police car on my daily commute, let alone a radar trap. Perhaps they find it too scary to be out on the roads, and I don't blame them.

If the French want to get serious about their accident rate, they should forget about cutting down trees and simply enforce the new law. This would lead to a wholesale confiscation of licenses and, within a month, the entire nation would be grounded. The rest of us would have the superb highways of France entirely to ourselves.

21

The Stevenson Trail

At about the age of twelve, I was captivated by a small book called *Travels with a Donkey in the Cévennes*. The author was the Scottish writer Robert Louis Stevenson, who is best remembered for those splendid adventure stories *Treasure Island,* and *Kidnapped,* and for the dark, Freudian fantasy of *Dr. Jekyll and Mr. Hyde.* But he was also a fine travel writer, and a passionate lover of France. *Travels with a Donkey* is an account of his eleven-day hike through one of the wildest and most beautiful parts of France, with an obstinate donkey called Modestine. I always longed to follow in Stevenson's footsteps. Now, after a fashion, I have.

Stevenson's journey, or rather the book he wrote about it, has spawned a whole industry. Many tourists in the Cévennes hire donkeys in order to relive his experience properly. I was all in favor of authenticity, but Diane refused to consider it. If I wanted to travel for eleven days on a donkey, she said, that was my problem. Needless to say we ended up driving along Stevenson's route in our little blue Citroen.

We began this modified adventure where Stevenson himself began, in the town of Monastier. It was once a prosperous center of the lace making industry, but was now so empty and gloomy that it might have been the very birthplace of Protestantism. The weather co-operated perfectly. It had been cold, dark and wet for Stevenson, and it was exactly the same for us.

Starting frFrom Monastier, Stevenson and Modestine walked a total distance of about a hundred and twenty miles. They were often lost, often misdirected by peasants, and they slept in horrible inns without cable TV or hot water. Sometimes they were forced to camp in the open, in the rain. Stevenson had plenty of time to think. Indeed, he traveled alone quite deliberately, so that he *could* think.

His was a type of journey almost forgotten: a philosophical journey. His mental companions were writers like Laurence Sterne, William Hazlitt and Henry David Thoreau. Not many tourists in the Cévennes today carry this kind of intellectual baggage. The journey unfolds on several levels. Stevenson was fascinated by the geography of the region, by the aesthetic quality of the landscape, and also by the religious character of the people who lived there. This was and is the heartland of French Protestantism, so its history interested the Scottish author very much. The light relief in the book was provided by the unfortunate donkey Modestine, their joint misadventures, and the people they met along the way.

This meditative experience of travel is precisely what we modern tourists miss. We move much too fast. Stevenson spent a whole difficult day walking from the village of Cheylard to the village of Luc, both of which he hated. It took us fifteen minutes to cover the same distance, and discover that he was right. A Citroen is not a donkey, and a national highway is not a footpath. when you are going at hundred kilometers an hour on mountain roads, and surrounded by French drivers, any form of meditation would be suicidal. And with hotel prices what they now are, we couldn't afford to linger and soak up the atmosphere of a place the way Stevenson did. His accommodation, when he could find it, cost about fifty cents a night, including meals. These rates have increased. Even a single night in a modest hotel in the Cévennes costs as much fifty donkeys at 1878 prices.

So although we followed Stevenson's route, and saw the same villages and landscapes that he saw more than a century ago, I can't pretend that we had any deep philosophical experiences as a result. But I'm glad we did it. The scenery was incomparable, and there was at least some sense of reliving a piece of history, even if at fast-forward.

The closest we came to a philosophical experience was right at the end of the road. Stevenson halted his journey and sold the much-abused Modestine in a pleasant village called St. Jean du Gard. Today, inevitably, there is now a Stevenson Tavern there, with tartan decorations and a selection of Scotch whiskies. When we walked in, we found a group of young men celebrating the fact that they had just walked the whole Stevenson trail. They were taking digital photos of one another wrapped in the tartan curtains. The French customers were completely mystified, until the whisper ran around the room: "They're from Scotland." Ah, said the customers philosophically, of course, and returned to their lunches. Modestine, something of a philosopher herself, would certainly have understood.

22

The Memory Man

There is a town not far from Chartres that has two names: one real, and one fictional. The fictional name, Combray, is familiar to lots of people because it appears in the vast novel by Marcel Proust, *Remembrance of Things Past*. The real name of the town is Illiers, and many thousands of people travel there each year to see if Illiers really is like Combray, much as people go to New York to see if it is identical to Gotham City in the Batman movies, which of course it is.

A strange mixture of people come to Illiers/Combray: professors of French literature from small colleges in the Midwest, neurotics, hypochondriacs, gays, former students who have vague memories of reading the Cliff Notes on Proust, and people like us driven by a vague conviction that we should make the pilgrimage to Illiers/Combray at least once in a lifetime.

We found a small, pleasant market town, almost embarrassed to be famous. There was very little commercialism or hype. This may be because so few people have actually read Proust's enormous classic, so it is hard to know what to hype. In Disneyland, for example, plastic mice and ducks are hot-selling items. But what kind of plastic souvenir can you make out of *Remembrance of Things Past,* which was written between 1912 and 1922 and fills seven thick books? The first volume alone contains more than five hundred closely printed pages. In essence it is an attempt to capture and relive the author's whole life by fixing it forever in words: approximately ten million words.

Small parts of it have been filmed, but the entire epic has never been made into a movie because it would take six months to watch. Even without a movie Proust is an icon of French literature, and his fame had recently been revived in America by Alain de Botton's ingenious self-help book, *How Proust Can Change Your Life*.

Remembrance of Things Past is certainly one of the most remarkable autobiographical novels ever written, but nobody could call it easy. I doggedly read the whole thing years ago, in an English translation. When we arrived in France I set myself the task of reading it in French. I failed, for two reasons: my French is so bad, and Proust's is so good. He has sentences that go on for three pages. He uses the most complex grammatical structures that the diabolical French language can provide.

Proust's autobiographical novel begins and ends with memory. Characteristically, the story begins on page fifty-one. In this famous passage he is already a grown man, living in Paris. His mother gives him some tea and a little shell-shaped cake called a *madeleine,* which he dips into the tea. The taste brings back the memory of his childhood in Combray, where his old Aunt Léonie would give him this very same treat. Then every vivid detail of his past life comes flooding back, and sets in motion the unstoppable narrative of the book. Here's just a fragment from that episode, in the classic translation by Scott Montcrieff and Terence Kilmartin.

"When from a long distant past nothing remains, after the people are dead, after the things are broken and scattered, taste and smell alone, more fragile but more enduring, more immaterial, more persistent, more faithful, remain poised for a long time, like souls, remembering, waiting, hoping, amid the ruins of all the rest; and bear unflinchingly, in the tiny and almost impalpable drop of their essence, the vast structure of recollection."

That's what I call a complex sentence: fourteen subordinate clauses, thirteen commas, and a semi-colon. It reads much better in French, but there weren't enough aspirins in Europe to get me through all seven volumes in the original.

In search of my own long-lost memories, I tried tasting a *madeleine*, dipping it in tea as prescribed. I tasted with my pen poised and half a dozen spare pens at the ready, because this very experience had launched Proust into a torrent of ten million words. The cake was delicious, but I remembered absolutely nothing. Diane pointed out that I had never tasted a *madeleine* in my life before, so I could hardly expect it open the floodgates of memory. I suspect this is one reason why Marcel Proust never married. He was a great literary genius with an inexhaustible fund of memories. He didn't need a critic.

23

The Tram to Odysseum

I've never been able to resist romantic place names. Once, driving down the Long Island Expressway, I was seduced by a sign to "Utopia Parkway." I followed it, hoping that perhaps utopia might be at the end of the road. It wasn't. My life has been full of these small geographical disappointments: Casablanca, Key West, Stratford on Avon, Troy—unromantic tourist traps, every one of them.

But, against all experience, I still hope that a destination will be as exotic as it sounds. So when in the city of Montpellier I saw a tram gliding by that had on its destination board the golden word "Odysseum," I jumped on board at once, without a ticket.

A minor argument with a tram driver seemed a small price to pay for a voyage to Odysseum. Odysseus was the hero of Homer's *Odyssey*, one of the great travel and adventure stories of all time. Jumping on a French tram without a ticket was exactly the sort of thing that Odysseus would have done. Somehow, in the destination of this tram, the name of Odysseus had been combined with the name of the Greek Paradise—Elysium—to form the infinitely enticing word Odysseum. How could anyone resist?

If Odysseus came to modern Montpellier, he would find himself in a strangely familiar landscape. The new part of town is a monumental tribute to Greek architecture and culture. The tram glides through streets called Acropolis, Poseidon, Rhodes, Athens, Mycenae and, oddly enough, one named after the satirical Roman poet Juvenal, who coined the phrase "Bread and circuses." Somebody slipped up there. The main shopping center is called Antigone, after the daughter of Oedipus, and even our waitress at lunch was named Sybil, like the Greek prophetess.

"You should have the fish," she said in an oracular fashion, and she was right.

The mayor of Montpellier since 1977, Georges Frêche, is one of the last of the old-time city bosses. He has presided over a positively imperial expansion of the city to its present size of almost a quarter of a million. The grandiose, Greek-inspired architecture is as impressive as anything in Europe. Everything on the east side of town looks brand new. This is how Chicago or Detroit must have looked in the boom decades of the 1870s and 1880s. Perhaps it's how Athens looked in 600BC, when speculative builders were throwing up new temples all over the place.

Through this surreal, postmodern landscape, the ultra-modern blue trams glide like something from a science fiction movie. Students love them, and indeed the trams offer an educational example of the intersection of technology and biology. Students who ride the trams regularly can get a discount card. Each time they board a tram they just wave the magnetic card at an electronic reader by the door, just below waist level. When it beeps, they can get on.

Montpellier is full of achingly beautiful young girls who have found a way to make the most of this system. They keep the magnetic cards in the back pockets of their very tight jeans. When they get on a tram they do a little dip, and wiggle their tiny bums at the magnetic reader until it beeps. The French boys adore this. Sometimes, they applaud!

The city of Montpellier won a European award for this tramway as model of urban transportation. Like all awards, this one is double-edged. Trams are a wonderfully cheap, efficient and environmentally friendly way to get around town. But they also encourage more development, more suburbs, and more people. In other words, transportation brings agglomeration, which the French call "Agglo." It's certainly happening in Montpellier, which is a high-tech boomtown. All the concrete and glass in Europe seems to be heading their way.

When my tram reached Odysseum, the end of the line, it was inevitably a bit of a disappointment. There was a car park, a huge building site, a multi-screen cinema, and the beginnings of a new suburban development. I didn't really expect anything else. As Odysseus himself might have said: "*C'est la vie.*"

24

Ship of Fools

The Mediterranean coast has astonishing birds: there are whole fields full of white egrets, and saltwater lakes full of flamingoes—curious, awkward birds, that should really only exist as garden decorations. We heard about what sounded like a wonderful excursion organized by a local ornithological society. They had hired a boat for a voyage on the Mediterranean to observe exotic sea birds—bring your own lunch, binoculars, and bird identification books. However, certain other essential items of equipment were not mentioned, such as thermal underwear, the complete works of Marcel Proust, and a very large bottle of brandy. We signed on without thought or hesitation and, at dawn on the appointed Sunday, we presented ourselves at the harbor carrying our borrowed binoculars and some sandwiches.

There were several things we had failed fully to appreciate about this trip. It was mid-winter, it was cold, it was even colder out on the ocean, and the boat had no source of heat.

Also, it was a much longer voyage than we had expected. We had somehow mis-translated the word "excursion," assuming that it implied a pleasant meander along a few miles of the coastline, where most birds are to be found. Instead, we headed straight out to sea, so far out that a landfall in Africa seemed a distinct possibility. At some invisible pre-determined spot the engines were stopped and we sat tossing on the ocean for six hours, throwing dead fish into an empty sky.

The other thing that we had not fully appreciated about this little adventure was what might be called the social or sociological aspect. In effect, we were cast adrift all day in an open boat with about a hundred fanatical French bird watchers. Nothing in our previous lives had prepared us for this.

Both Diane and I are interested in birds, but neither of us is a "bird watcher," in the sense of someone who will spend all night in a swamp waiting for a Black Tailed Godwit. But these folks were serious. They carried binoculars of astronomical dimensions, cameras with lenses three feet long, and notebooks. As soon as the boat stopped, they established themselves in advantageous positions from stem to stern, some balanced on seats, others kneeling precariously on top of the wheelhouse. The sea was uninhabited from horizon to horizon, and we all waited as bucket after bucket of fish vanished over the side in a vain attempt to attract birds. It was like a fishing expedition in reverse.

Hours passed. At last, a herring gull appeared. This is the ordinary gull that you can see by the thousands in any harbor. Soon we were surrounded by a cloud of gulls. The bird watchers, their enthusiasm fired by all this avian activity, began to imagine that they could spot other birds. Somebody would point to a tiny speck on the horizon, crying: "It's a Razorbill," and they would all rush dangerously to that side of the boat, lenses aimed like so many cannons in a Napoleonic Man of War. "Non, non," somebody else would claim, "It's a Gannett." Usually, it would turn out to be another gull, or an "unconfirmed" sighting of something extremely rare. I was tempted to raise the cry of "Albatross" but, in this company, it would have been the equivalent of shouting "Fire" in a crowded theater. Bird identification would be far more reliable and far less stressful if birds carried their names on their bodies, like commercial aircraft.

I will spare you all the excruciating details. We did see a few Cormorants, remarkably like those in Bridgeport or Port Jefferson. We did return to land at last, almost paralyzed with cold and boredom. But the bird watchers were happy. Their notebooks were full of more or less imaginary birds, and the expedition was counted a great success.

As we tottered off the boat, and headed in the direction of the nearest warm café, they smiled and said: "Until next time."

That's another thing that every bird watcher needs: a sense of humor.

25

Who Loves Paris?

We were fortunate, I think, to be living within easy reach of Paris. Whenever we got tired of village life we could just empty the bank account, take a high-speed train from Montpellier, and be at the *Gare d'Austerlitz* in four hours. Everybody claims to love Paris. They love it in the summer, when it sizzles, and even in the winter, when it drizzles—which it certainly does. But, after our last visit, I found myself in a minority of one. I didn't love Paris any more.

This is not the city's fault—it is still one of the most beautiful in the world. The streets and buildings are probably authentic, although one can never be quite sure. But no city in history had been so over-praised, over-romanticized, and over-sold as Paris. Rome had pretensions, in the great days of the Caesars, and modern New York is famous for its grandstanding claims to be the world's greatest city. But, when it comes to hype and hyperbole, no place compares to Paris.

Paris is the single most popular tourist destination on the planet, hosting an estimated seventy million French and foreign visitors every year. Six million of them find it necessary to climb the Eiffel Tower. Jumbo jets full of Japanese, Americans and Australians come roaring into Charles de Gaulle airport every few minutes. Since the Channel Tunnel was built, the British have spearheaded the biggest invasion since the Hundred Years War. Fast European express trains bring more tourists in from everywhere. It is even rumored that a few brave souls have *driven* to Paris, although they were never heard from again.

This tells the visitor what to expect. Paris is not a primarily French experience, or a cultural experience, or even a romantic experience: it is an international tourist experience. Even in mid-winter the sidewalks were blocked by gawping sightseers, clutching maps and bottles of spring water, the charming restaurants resounded with the twanging accents of Manchester, Milwaukee or Melbourne, and every major exhibition or show attracted a line of foreigners that stretched around the block.

The Parisians themselves were almost invisible. In fact, they are moving out of the city as fast as they can. In a poll taken in 2001, *La Parisienne* magazine revealed that six out of ten Parisians want to leave the place entirely. They are moving to smaller cities and country towns with less crowding, less traffic, fewer tourists, less outrageous property prices, and above all less crime. Those who must keep jobs in Paris are commuting up to two hundred miles on high-speed trains, just so they don't have to live there.

Here is a case where Monsieur Disney and his team of clever illusionists could actually do some good. Euro Disney is already flourishing just outside Paris. Why not return the compliment, and build a Parisian theme park in America? Disney's magicians-in-plastic could reproduce Paris in some convenient empty location—perhaps Kansas. They could sell cheap flights and a single bargain-price ticket to cover all the attractions, including a fake Eiffel Tower, a fake Louvre with a fake Mona Lisa, a fake Metro without the beggars, and a fake French dinner at a fake Arpège. They could also provide plenty of public bathrooms. The real Paris would become a delightful city again, and the real Parisians could come out of hiding and live there.

It's always a shame when cities or even villages are depopulated just because they are so popular. Too many tourists make any place unlivable, and it becomes nothing but a historic monument. Take Stonehenge, for example, or Machu Pichu, where the locals were driven out by hordes of visitors centuries ago.

That is the sad fate of Paris today. It has become a theme park, a monument to what it used to be. We're never going there again—or at least not until our trip in the Spring. We wouldn't want to miss Paris in the Spring.

26

A Modest Proposal

Spring brought the tourists flocking back to the south of France like swallows returning to San Capistrano. The roads were suddenly full of little Dutch caravans going at forty miles an hour, and big Mercedes with Swiss plates going at a hundred and ten.

Tourism is the continuation of war by other means. The history of Europe had been an endless succession of wars and invasions. The French struggled mightily to keep out the British in 1453, and succeeded. They struggled to keep out the Germans in 1914 and 1939, and failed. Now there are places in France where practically the only languages you hear spoken are English and German.

Tourism has many advantages over outright war. It's far less violent, and somewhat less damaging to the environment. It has also been very good for the French economy. Instead of fighting to keep us foreigners out, they welcome us in and sell us hotel rooms, meals, wines, expensive museum tickets and overpriced souvenirs. The old enemies have become valued customers.

A particularly vivid illustration of this is the walled town called Aigues-Mortes (dead waters, in the local dialect) that rests darkly on the salt flats beside the Mediterranean. Aigues-Mortes was built by Louis IX in the 13th century. For eight hundred years this grim fortress stood impregnable against all invaders. Now the moat is bridged and the massive main gate is wide open. You can walk right in, after paying an exorbitant parking fee, and all the invaders in the world are inside the walls, busily buying t-shirts and eating pizzas.

Tourism is good. It's based on a healthy instinct to escape from everyday life and to see new things, and it makes the world a safer place. What troubles me is the *unfairness* of it all. Some of us always seem to be traveling, and others always seem to be working in the tourist industry, seeing nothing more exciting than the inside of a kitchen or an airport. Reliable authorities have said that all men and women are created equal, and this doesn't seem to be a very equalitarian arrangement.

Nobody likes to work, but everyone likes to travel. So it seems obvious that the world's population should be divided into two more or less equal groups, with (say) names from A to M in one group and N to Z in the other. For the first year, the A to Ms would be perpetual tourists, traveling the world and viewing its wonders according to their various whims. The N to Zs would slave away in the tourist industry, running the hotels and manufacturing those nasty souvenirs.

At the end of the year, everyone would switch. The N to Zs would grab their passports and stomach pills and start traveling, the A to Ms would get to work in the bars, bistros, and theme parks. All other kinds of work not connected to tourism would cease. Thus one half of the world would always be helping the other half to have a good time, and they would understand one another's problems. Terrorists and fanatics would be calmed down by weeks relaxing on the beach, or exhausted by walking around museums. Even the Taliban might relax a bit after a long vacation in the south of France. Politicians would become entirely redundant. They could be put to work making suntan oil and other slippery substances.

Economists predict that tourism will soon be the world's biggest industry. We may as well take the next logical step and make it the world's *only* industry.

27

Misguided Tours

During our visit to Italy we stayed on a farm in the Tuscan countryside The landscape was so like a Renaissance painting that we scarcely dared to drive into it for fear of ripping the canvas. It was quiet, it was idyllic, and we could walk for miles without encountering another human being.

But, as everyone knows, it is a violation of the rules of international tourism to visit that part of Italy without going to Florence. So we did. Florence has never been a peaceful place. Julius Caesar founded the city 59 B.C. as a fortress against the primitive northern tribes. The northern tribes keep coming, even today, and still cause trouble in the gift shops. From the eleventh to the seventeenth century, Florence was regularly torn apart by internal power struggles, fought over by Tuscans, Romans and Lombards, and oppressed by rulers who were less than one hundred per cent democratic such as the Médici and Savonarola. Machiavelli was a typical product of Florentine politics. In 1797, Florence was annexed by Napoleon, and it was bitterly fought over in World War Two. Then the tourists came.

After an absence of some years we had forgotten just how many tourists could be crammed into this small city. Florence has some of the greatest art and architectural treasures of the world and, even though we were there midweek and out of season, it seemed as if the whole world had come to see them on the same day. We added our own small contribution to the crowding problem, the parking problem, and the pollution problem, when we should have stayed in the country.

The streets were literally choked with compact masses of people, each group shuffling along, shoulder-to-shoulder led by a tour guide with a flag or some kind of symbol held aloft. We saw one tour led by a man with an ear of corn on a stick, presumably a delegation from Iowa. These groups moved steadily ahead regardless of obstacles, including us. In some streets there was nothing to be seen but a mass of bobbing backpacks. The line outside the Uffizi Gallery was half a mile long, and the electronic counter inside the door of the Duomo showed that it had almost reached its maximum capacity of eight hundred people. Overhead, jumbo jets laden with more tourists were droning into Amerigo Vespucci airport every few minutes. When we wanted to take photographs we had to wait until a gap in the crowd revealed a piece of actual scenery, then take a shot quickly without worrying too much what it was.

If you wanted a picture of yourself in front of some famous monument the local street photographers were happy to oblige. They used digital cameras to create a montage of your image standing in front of an empty scene.

A lot of the visitors were high school students from all over the world enjoying an educational tour. "Enjoying" and "educational" may both be the wrong words to use here. I've not seen so many bored, unhappy and rebellious young people gathered together in one place since the last time I taught a college class. The only things that seemed to attract their attention were the pizza and ice cream stands, video game arcades, and Internet cafes, which were strategically placed along the main tourist routes. These so-called educational tours may be fun for the teachers, although their haggard faces make me doubt it. I'm certain that they are counter-productive for the students, who probably learn only to detest beauty and culture for the rest of their lives.

"They say that travel broadens the mind," wrote G.K.Chesterton, "But first you must have the mind."

It made me glad that my old school never offered anything as fancy as educational tours. As a teenager I got a tremendous kick out of doing Europe on my own—arriving in Rome by motor cycle from London at age seventeen. I knew nothing about Rome after 400 A.D., when the history in our school textbook ended. But my visit was all the more memorable because of more recent developments, which came as a surprise.

I have very mixed feelings about mass tourism, because I'm a part of it. Everybody should be able to see unique and wonderful places like Florence. But, with six billion people in the world, we can't do it without destroying the places we want to see. We felt doubly guilty because both of us had been to Florence before so we really didn't have to go again. Just to compound the felony we later drove to Venice, where the crowds were ten times worse. Soon they will need pushers, like those on the Tokyo subway, just to shove people into Venice. In short, Italy is full. They must do something to control the crowds. The Greeks have the neat idea of reducing traffic in Athens by allowing drivers to enter the city only on alternate days, based on their license plate numbers. Florence could use a similar system, perhaps based on nationality: Germans on Tuesdays and Thursdays, Americans on Wednesdays and Saturdays, and so on.

Travel agents could help to rationalize mass tourism by exercising a little discretion at the point of sale. A few simple questions such as: "Do you like to stand in line for five hours to see a lot of very large, very dark religious paintings by artists who died four hundred years ago, or do you prefer to play Blackjack?" would help to distinguish the people who would enjoy Florence from those who would have a better time in Las Vegas. But, like all brilliantly simple solutions, this one will never be implemented. Only Savonarola could solve the problem of tourists in Florence.

Charles Baudelaire captured the spirit of tourism in poetry much better than I can say it in prose. Here's a free translation of Baudelaire's poem, "*Voyageurs*" (Travellers):

The true tourists are those who leave just in order to leave;
Their hearts are as light as balloons,
They never shrink from their fate,
But, without knowing why, simply say "Let's go."

28

A Universal Language

One of the many pleasures of living in France is that Italy is just around the corner. It's easier and less stressful to drive from the south of France to Italy than from eastern Long Island to Kennedy airport—and Italy has plenty of free parking.

When you cross a European frontier, everything changes—the language, the lifestyle and, in some mysterious way, even the landscape. In the United States, just because they are more or less united, the traveler doesn't experience the same cultural shocks. You can cross from New York into Connecticut, for example, and not notice the difference for days, or even for years. If you cross from France into Italy you drive into a completely different world.

It's true that, since the coming of the European Community, frontier crossings aren't as dramatic as they used to be. Thirty years ago the formalities were quite daunting. In addition to a passport, and often a visa, you had to carry customs documents for the vehicle, a special certificate of insurance, an International Driver's License, and an authorization from your bank to exchange currencies. Now the frontiers are truly open. We zipped out of France and past the sign that said "Welcome to Italy" in half a dozen languages, without ever dropping below seventy miles an hour.

Italy is always a treat. Before the Euro came along you become an instant millionaire as soon as you exchanged your currency. One Italian lira was worth approximately one twentieth of one American cent. A tank full of gas cost 75,000 lira. It made a person feel rich, but also dizzy from trying to count all the zeroes. One night, in a hotel, we watched the Italian version of "Who Wants to be a Millionaire?" But a million lire were worth about five hundred dollars, so it had to be called "Who wants to be a Billionaire?"

I've lived on Long Island for so long that I feel half Italian already, so I launched into speech with great confidence. There is a certain point in learning any language where you know virtually nothing, but imagine that you know quite a lot. That was and is the state of my Italian: a couple of minutes with the phrase book, and I'm ready for conversation on any subject, especially food. The great thing about the Italians is that, unlike the French, they play along with your illusion that you are speaking some recognizable version of their language, and even try their best to help.

The differences between the nations of Europe are slowly disappearing. The Italians have lost the prodigal lira in exchange for the Euro. A thousand old lira equals about three Euros, so arithmetic is much easier. The French are forgetting the franc, the Germans have mothballed the mark, and all prices are quoted in Euros. It makes sense, but it's dull.

Europe already had a universal food, pizza; a universal juvenile headgear, the backward baseball cap; and a universal television hero, Bart Simpson. Starting in 2002 the nations of the European Community have a universal currency`. The next logical step must surely be a universal language that will make the union of Europe as solid as that of the United States.

A lot of people, especially the British, want that language to be English, but I'd vote for Italian. After all, it is the direct descendant of the Latin that was spoken all over Europe two thousand years ago. It is the language of Dante, the language of Grand Opera, and the familiar language of a million Long Island restaurant menus. Italian is so clear, logical, and pronounceable, that I believe even I could learn it. If Italian became the universal language of Europe I might stand a better chance of being understood, in France.

Part IV

ADVENTURES IN FRENCH CULTURE

29

Local Hero

The British have not been welcome in France since the Hundred Years War, and Americans are even less popular. As a British/American couple, we anticipated a certain amount of coolness or even hostility from our new neighbors. We thought about pretending to be Canadians, or even Australians. But honesty prevailed, and we presented ourselves in Aniane under our true colors. We came prepared to apologize for just about everything, from the English victory in the Battle of Agincourt in 1415 to the tax on Roquefort cheese that America imposed in the year 2000.

We needn't have worried. The British are regarded as a joke, and Americans are treated as gigantic children There was no overt anti-Americanism. But gigantic children can be dangerous. There is an uneasy feeling that huge out-of-control American corporations are taking over the world, and that the French are powerless to do anything about it.

Wine-making is the main industry in the Languedoc. Most of the vineyards are owned by French companies or by local families, and their wines are just beginning to get an international reputation. Naturally, they want to expand. But capital is scarce and, in this mountainous area, so is good growing land. Most of the remaining forests are strictly protected against agricultural development.

Into this quiet rural scene stomped a gigantic child: the big Californian wine maker Mondavi, looking for a place to create a prestige wine with a French label. Mondavi wanted to plant about seven hundred acres of protected forest with vines. None of the local wine makers had been able to get permission to do this, but local politicians came to an "understanding" with the American company which allowed them to go ahead. The local growers naturally saw this as an unfair land-grab by an American monster with unlimited capital that would eventually wipe them off the map.

In France, globalization usually means Americanization. The local hero of the anti-globalization campaign was a farmer and activist called José Bové, who once made a sledgehammer attack on a half-built McDonald's restaurant in the town of Millau, not far from Aniane. He was sentenced to jail for three months for this escapade, amid massive protest demonstrations by his many supporters. In August 2001, out of jail, Bové was back outside the MacDonalds in Millau with 20,000 supporters to protest *la malbouffe americaine* (American garbage food).

McDonald's, which the French call "McDo," had become a symbol of globalisation. The whole landscape of France is disfigured by golden arches. In beautiful cities like Montpellier, the ugly red and yellow advertising is in your face wherever you look. My favorite sidewalk café in Paris is now a McDonald's. The farmers represented by José Bové see this as the thin end of a very large wedge, which includes genetically modified crops, industrial agriculture, international food marketing, and punitive American import taxes on French exports like cheese and *foie gras*. For them, it's not just French farming that's at stake, but French culture.

French children eat American fast food and consume American movies, TV shows and video games in enormous quantities. They are becoming Americans, just as the nations conquered by the Romans two thousand years ago eventually saw their children become little Romans. That's the penalty for being the most powerful nation: you are admired, feared, imitated, and always resented.

On the day before the 2000 Presidential election, the newspaper *Le Monde* published the results of a public opinion survey. French citizens were asked what they thought were the outstanding characteristics of America. Their answers, in order, were: 1. Uncontrolled firearms; 2. The death penalty; 3. Restrictive abortion laws; 4. Racism; 5. Lack of affordable health care; 6. Child poverty; 7. The power of big business; 8. Excessive working hours; and 9. Religious fanaticism. On the positive side, American video games were admitted to be very good.

The McDonald's that José Bové tried to demolish with his sledgehammer is now repaired, and doing a brisk business. But no quantity of burgers, pickles and fries can entirely overcome the resentment of American economic power. The slogan of Bové's political movement is everywhere: painted along the highways, one word at a time, and even high up on the sides of mountains.

"*Le monde n'est pas une marchandise.*"

"The world is not for sale."

It's a great slogan: too bad it's not true.

30

Long Live the Difference

The French are very proud of their commitment to sexual equality. Women are half the workforce, and are major players in politics. A law passed in 2001 requires that fifty per-cent of candidates for local and European elections must be women. The only problem with this law so far has been finding enough women foolish enough to stand for political office in the first place.

Men like to complain that "Women make all the decisions in France." Frenchmen have been saying this ever since the time of Catherine de Médici and Marie-Antoinette, and it may even be true. In the streets and cafes of the city, in business and the professions, women seem confident and even dominant. They somehow manage to appear serious and capable, while at the same time remaining elegant, and very feminine. On the face of it, French women have achieved the best of both worlds, equality with personal freedom. As they themselves might say, if they had my command of the language, *vive la différence*.

But sexual equality was less obvious in a village like Aniane. Relationships between women and men seemed stuck in another century. In some ways, it was recognizably the world of Marcel Proust, or even of Flaubert. The men hung out in bars, they hunted, they drank, and they played games The young boys with their motorcycles gathered on a corner at the opposite end of the village, beside the Pavillion bar. The women had no public gathering place, except the general store of Monsieur Vidal. They cooked and cleaned and took care of children. While the men loudly occupied public spaces, the women stayed indoors, or stood isolated on their balconies. Traditional men in traditional villages have a hard time adjusting to the notion of sexual equality.

What started me thinking about this sensitive topic was a newspaper article recalling the fact that Simone de Beauvoir had died in Paris fifteen years before. She's a historic figure now, and her name may not be so familiar to the younger generation. But it was Beauvoir who launched French feminism in 1949 with her book *The Second Sex*. I can't claim that Beauvoir changed my life, but she certainly changed part of my mind. I've never forgotten her passionate diatribe against the myth of femininity since I first read it many years ago

Beauvoir wrote: "One is not born but is made a woman," meaning that femininity, like masculinity, was something you learned, much the same way you learned your own language, without even knowing it. The trouble with femininity, she argued, was that it prevented women from ever competing with men on an equal basis.

The Second Sex was too intellectual to make much of a popular impact. But the message that came through was a passionate plea to reject what she called the myth of femininity—that women were different and more delicate. Women were just like men, she argued. They thought the same thoughts, and wanted the same things. This was news to me. In 1949 it was news to just about everybody.

So French women were way ahead in the first wave of feminism. But they lost political ground by being rather too sophisticated. Following Beauvoir, French feminism has been complicated, thoughtful, literary, historical, and philosophical. Issues like equal pay were not the cutting edge. But ordinary French women didn't want to be the same as men, or to reject men. They just wanted women to have a better deal as women, without pretending to be something else.

I'm not foolish enough to take sides in the eternal argument about whether women and men can be equal but different, in France or anywhere else. More than half a century after the publication of *The Second*

Sex, the French often do seem to achieve that delicate balance between equality and difference. In spite of all the conflicts and changes women and men seem to take real pleasure in each other's company, and in the innocent game of flirtation which political correctness has almost killed in America.

No balance is perfect. The old French habit of the extra-marital affair seems as strong as ever although, according to recent research, women now participate on a basis of full equality. The top levels of government, the civil service and business are still totally dominated by gray, middle aged men. But this may be because French women are too smart to throw away their lives on such trivial pursuits.

However, this may change with the constitutional amendment of 2001. In future elections, there will be just as many women candidates as men, and more than fifty per cent of French voters are women. If that doesn't work to increase the numbers of women elected, it's hard to imagine what will.

This kind of artificial, merely political equality is not at all what Simone de Beauvoir had in mind. She wanted nothing less than a cultural and psychological revolution—and it may be happening, even in Aniane. On weekends, the boys outside the Pavillion bar were joined by a few young women. Some of them even had their own motorcycles—serious motorcycles, not those silly little machines that sound like angry mosquitoes. Half a century ago Beauvoir raged against femininity as a myth, and a strait jacket for women. She would probably approve of the young women bikers of Aniane in their leather jackets as the scruffy vanguard of a new and more assertive style of French womanhood.

Once village girls start riding big motorcycles, and hanging out in bars—in other words, acting just as badly as boys—full equality and a female President cannot be too far away.

31

Love in a Warm Climate

No nation has a more romantic image than France. When it comes to love, the French have the enviable reputation of being the all-time world champions. America excels at business, Britain is proud of its history, and Australia had many peculiar animals. But only France claims romantic love as its special, national genius.

The reasons for this were not immediately obvious to us, at least not in Aniane in February. It was dark, it was chilly, it was often wet, and the villagers spent most of their time indoors. When they did venture out they were wrapped in five layers of shapeless clothing. It was hard to imagine even the basic continuation of the species under these conditions, let alone romantic encounters of the Charles Boyer kind.

There is some real evidence for this apparent lack of sexual charisma. Professor John Gagnon of the State University of New York at Stony Brook recently published a study purporting to prove that the French are nowhere near as sexually active or adventurous as they are imagined (and imagine themselves) to be. In fact, they are about as boring in this department as Americans. This research caused horror and outrage throughout France—it was even reported on the front page of *Le Figaro*. Could it be true? On Valentine's Day, the inhabitants of Aniane certainly gave the impression that romance was the last thing on their minds.

Perhaps Valentine's Day is not a fair test of France's romantic image. Spring is the season for romance. Valentine's Day comes at completely the wrong time of year, when roses are impossibly expensive and long before a young man's fancy lightly turns to thoughts of love. In France, in February, most young men have only one thing on their minds—hunting. They spend all day and half the night out on the mountain with their guns, looking for wild boar. Romance doesn't stand a chance, at least not until the hunting season ends on February twenty-eighth.

Valentine's Day was therefore a bit of a non-event. We didn't see a single heart-shaped chocolate box, Madame Georgette the florist took the whole thing very calmly, and Madame Lily's boutique had no special Valentine's cards. In terms of sheer expenditure, America is more romantic by far—the entire country is awash in hearts and flowers for weeks ahead. In America, Valentine's Day is not just for couples but for friends, relatives, domestic animals, and even children who exchange Valentines in school. The French express unbelieving horror at this very kinky behavior.

I asked the young lady in the village beauty salon about Valentine's Day while she was cutting my hair. It's nothing special, she said. It's a day for couples, and why would you send a card to somebody who is living in the same house? Everybody agreed: this is a day dedicated to people who are married, or almost married. The restaurants do a brisk business, and that's about it.

This makes perfect sense if we go back to the origins of Valentine's Day. St. Valentine was a priest, martyred by the Emperor Claudius on 14th February in the year 270, for the crime of celebrating Christian marriages, which were forbidden at the time. So, according to the history, Valentine's Day is really all about family values rather than the wilder shores of romance.

Which leaves the question: just how romantic are the French? Does their reputation depend entirely on a sexy accent and a bunch of old Hollywood stereotypes? Is it the fact that French men still like to keep mistresses, or that French women—perhaps for this reason—are the world's primary consumers of exotic lingerie? How do you measure romance anyway? America comes out way ahead in the consumption of flowers, cards and chocolates.

But it is impossible to live in France without observing the small everyday gallantries, the undisguised interest that men and women take in each other, the trouble they take with their appearance every day, and their constant habit of touching and kissing. Even my elegant French teacher Madame Patricia once gave me three kisses, in spite of the chronic irregularity of my verbs. In Montpellier, delicious young girls stroll through the streets wearing t-shirts printed front and back with their e-mail addresses. The shirts are worn unusually tight, so that the addresses are easier to read.

Certain things are destined to remain a mystery. But I had the definite impression that, in France, it's Valentine's Day every day.

32

Toreador

Bullfighting upsets a lot of people, in France and abroad. It upsets me. When Madame Patricia invited me to write a short essay on this topic for my French homework, I turned in a piece so passionate, so full of adjectives, and even subjunctives, that she was quite shocked.

Bullfighting is really a Spanish vice. But it also exists in the southwestern corner of France, close to the Spanish border. In a typical week there were half a dozen *Corridas*. The word sounds so jolly and romantic. It makes you think of the Toreador song from Bizet's opera "Carmen." The advertising posters show graceful toreadors, dressed in operatic costumes. In the local paper a third of the sports pages were filled with reports and pictures from *La Corrida*, alongside the football scores and the racing results. It was some consolation that most of the pictures showed toreadors being chased over the barriers by infuriated bulls.

These same bulls can be seen grazing peacefully in the countryside along the edge of the Carmargue, where they are raised for the ring. It's clear that they intend nobody any harm, and would just like a quiet life. But their destiny is to be taken to the arena, kept in the dark until the last moment, pushed out into the blinding sunlight, and poked and prodded to death by the young toreador and his assistants, to the roaring approval of the crowd.

My opinions about bullfighting are firmly based on complete ignorance. I have never been to a live bullfight. For all I know it may be a heart-warming demonstration of kindness to animals. But, like everyone else, I've seen the videos and the movies, I've read Hemmingway, I've listened to "Carmen" dozens of time: that's more than enough.

The closest I ever came to the real thing was when we visited the magnificent Roman arena in Arles. In this very place, men and beasts have fought for over two thousand years. The Romans gave the advantage to the beasts; today's bullfighters give themselves much better odds. There was no bullfight on that particular day, and we bought twenty franc tickets to see the arena. The ring was surprisingly small and, sitting there in the winter sun, it was hard to imagine that they really did fight bulls out there on that patch of sand. But they do.

The vast majority of French people are against bullfighting, just as the majority of the English are against fox hunting. The French toreador, Richard Milian, describes the *corrida* as "An art, a spectacle of excitement and beauty." On the other side, a spokesman for the French League for Animal Rights describes it as "A monstrous torture, and an obscene spectacle that debases everyone involved." Not much chance of a happy compromise there.

There is some good news. There are two types of bullfighting in the Languedoc: the traditional Spanish *Corrida* just described, and a far less brutal event called the *Course à la Cocarde*. In this version the bulls are smaller and more docile. They have—and this must be embarrassing for them—a *Cocarde* or bunch of ribbons attached to their horns, which the young matadors must try to remove without getting gored or trampled. In these events, the bulls are rarely hurt.

Nobody will ever persuade me to attend real bullfight. But I might enjoy an afternoon watching the *Course à la Cocarde*. You can guess whose side I'll be on.

33

Loft Story

When America was focused on the Fourth of July last year, France was focused on the Fifth. This was not a great patriotic celebration for the French but a great media event, almost comparable to the cultural earthquake created in America by the last episode of Seinfeld in 1998.

"Loft Story" came to an end on Thursday, July 5, 2001. If this news leaves you completely cold, it's because you didn't have to live with the "Loft Story" phenomenon for three months, as we did. In brief, "Loft Story" was a television series, based on the original Dutch version of "Big Brother." The title (which was indeed in English, not French) referred to an artificial environment or "loft" which was constructed by the commercial television company M6 in a suburb outside Paris. Eleven young people—aged 20 to 29 but mentally much younger—were placed into this loft, or cage, to be studied night and day by television cameras for the titillation of the TV audience.

The experiment was so enormously successful that it stunned its own producers, and created a huge backlash of anger and criticism. I have never seen so much negative media coverage given to a TV program. Major newspapers and magazines carried lengthy discussions of "Loft Story," not just at the beginning of the show but week after week, month after month. I kept a file of these articles, which grew to the thickness of a club sandwich. I also persuaded myself (but not Diane) to watch the program itself three times, which was more than enough. After a while, I started asking everyone we met: "Have you watched 'Loft Story'?" Most of them looked shifty, and denied it. But the figures showed that most French households had tuned in, at least occasionally.

"Loft Story" aired every night at 7 p.m. to an average audience of six millions, with a two hour special on Thursdays. The eleven young people originally in the loft were slowly eliminated, by their own choice or by being voted out by viewers, until only the most brainless and beautiful were left. Their entire lives were on camera, including their sex lives and their visits to the bathroom. Naturally they became instant mega-celebrities. This helps to explain their huge appeal to the 15-24 age group who were their biggest fans. At that age, you believe that celebrity equals happiness. But, before the invention of "reality television," an aspiring celebrity had to do something—become a singer, or a writer, or master a sport or an art—but do *something*. The denizens of the loft became national celebrities simply by being on TV, and carrying on like a bunch of not very bright teenagers. In short, they became celebrities just by being themselves. It was irresistible. In terms of audience share "Loft Story" wiped all competing programs off the map.

The nature of the media criticism was interesting. It wasn't so much moral disapproval as intellectual outrage. "Loft Story" was accused of distracting viewers from more serious public TV channels, lambasted for dumbing down the medium, and reproached for degrading the audience and the subjects. Some critics, like Franco Bottiglioni, father in law of one of the lofters, pointed the finger back at intellectuals themselves. They had destroyed all values and inhibitions. How could they have the nerve complain about the result?

The lofters did what was expected of them. Their lives in the television fishbowl were filled with little dramas of love and jealousy. It would have been marvelous if they had rebelled—for example disappointing all their viewers by forming a study group, and spending the evenings reading and discussing ideas. But that would have been too much to hope for.

I can't tell you the end of the "Loft Story" story because I didn't watch the final episode. But, frankly, who cares? This was just about the most tasteless program ever created by a tasteless medium. The French, the nation of Descartes and Pascal, should be ashamed of themselves. The interesting thing is that they *are* ashamed of themselves.

34

Alternative Literature

Aniane has no bookstore, although satellite TV is very popular. But the nearby city of Montpellier, a big cultural and university center, has enough bookstores to satisfy the most avid reader in any language. All these bookstores, including the most classy intellectual establishments, sell comic books.

"Comic books" is the only term we have in English for this quintessentially French phenomenon. In fact they are just illustrated stories, which may not be comical at all. The French call them, *Bandes Dessinées,* literally "drawn strips," or "BDs" for short. The politically correct label is "Graphic Novels."

They are typically about fifty pages long, and embrace the whole range of conventional literature: science fiction, horror, westerns, detectives, and improbably exotic romances, as well as history and classics. The artwork is often original, and sometimes quite brilliant. Most contemporary art looks deadly dull by comparison. Indeed the artists are as famous as their characters, and the BDs are enjoyed by people of all ages. They are seriously reviewed as literature and as art, they appear in the bestseller lists alongside conventional novels, and they have their own international show at Angoulême every year.

My first thought on seeing all these comic books was: this is really dumb, how can people read this stuff? My second thought was: these could really help me with my French. The vocabulary seemed to consist largely of the international cartoon language that I had learned in childhood: "ZAP! POW! ZING! CRUNCH! BONG!" and so on. I was having a hard time reading Proust, but these cartoons I could understand. So I walked out of a bookstore with my very first volume of BD, carefully wrapped.

When you are launching into a whole new genre of literature, it's best to start at the top. So I had bought the newly published thirty-first volume in the adventures of Astérix the Gaul. Creator and artist Albert Uderzo invented Astérix in 1959, since when his books have sold three hundred million copies, and have been translated into 107 languages. The other great French cartoon heroes, the boy detective Tintin, the cowboy Lucky Luke, and the eternal loser Gaston Lagaffe, don't even come close.

The latest volume in the Astérix saga was called "Astérix and Latraviata". This seems to suggest a musical theme but, without giving away too much of the plot, I can reveal that music has nothing at all to do with it. Astérix is the perfect French hero, a symbol of national pride. His adventures are set at the height of the Roman Empire, when Rome had effectively colonized the territory that is now France. Astérix is a tiny warrior with a big blond mustache and a winged helmet. His much larger companion Obélix has long red hair, a big nose, and a huge stomach. The two of them always find a way to defend their little Gallic village against the four Roman legions that surround it.

Astérix is a superhero, but not in the style of Batman or Superman. *They* fight against mysterious individual enemies. Astérix takes on a whole foreign culture, personified by Caesar. In other words, like so much of French culture, Astérix is political. The Roman Empire has been dead for two thousand years, but the French still imagine that they see the triumphal arches of an alien empire everywhere, and they love to think in metaphors. It is interesting to speculate which imperial power, in the French imagination, has replaced Rome, and which mighty leader has replaced Caesar.

35

Strike of the Day

Labor Day happens on May 1 in France, as in most of Europe. It's the traditional May Day celebration of work and workers.

May Day is a big event, because France has such a strong socialist tradition. Oddly enough, in spite of this tradition, only ten per cent of French workers belong to a union, the lowest figure in the west. But those are unionized, mainly public sector workers, make the most of it. The whole point of being a public employee, in their view, is that you *can* go on strike and you *should* go on strike at every possible opportunity, just to show the government who's boss. After all, in the public sector, what difference can it possibly make?

It made a difference to us. It was disconcerting to walk to the post office and find the doors closed, or to drive to the train station and find no trains running. But it happened all the time. That's why we always studied the local paper before setting foot outside the house, to learn about the strike of the day.

Soon after we arrived in Aniane I began to keep a file on all the strikes. But it became too unwieldy to manage without secretarial help, so I can offer only the merest sketch of strikes that affected us down in the southwestern corner of France.

We arrived to a gasoline strike that paralyzed the whole country for two weeks. We had airline strikes, bus strikes, tram strikes, and ferry strikes. The entire French rail system was shut down just in time for the Easter vacation. Various supermarkets and big stores closed for days or weeks, along with the post office, and some banks. Social security workers and then the entire local civil service went on strike. One day we opened the newspaper and found a blank space where the weather forecast should have been—the forecasters were on strike. Hospital workers, gynecologists, schoolteachers, head teachers, the local police, student nurses, and tobacconists all went on strike during the same few short months. There were massive strikes in public and private industries in support of early retirement. The University of Montpellier, staff and students stayed on strike for a whole semester. Circus workers went on strike in the middle of winter, and those clowns blocked several main roads with their trucks. In the past two years the number of days lost to strikes has risen by sixty per cent.

My favorite strike story appeared just before Christmas. The unemployed threatened to go on strike to support their demand for larger Christmas bonuses. We speculated about how the unemployed *could* go on strike. Would they refuse to hang out in cafés? Would they refuse to play *pétanque* all day? We were quite disappointed when this particular strike failed to happen.

The legal system was not immune. We were amazed to see strikes by both judges and defense attorneys. This must seem very strange to lawyers in America. Why voluntarily cut down on your own billable hours, just when the boating season is coming up? The answer is that a great many French attorneys are employed by the state, and very badly paid. The nearest they ever get to boating is a rented rowing boat on the lake in the park.

All through April there was a nationwide strike of midwives. They are known by the rather quaint title of "Wise Women," which gave the local newspaper the opportunity for the headline: "Wise Women do Dumb Things." The midwives were demanding more professional recognition rather than more money, which seemed very reasonable. But it must have been a worrying strike for anyone who happened to be eight and three quarter months pregnant. A group of Kurds, asking for political asylum, went on hunger strike for two weeks, attracting massive publicity. When people land on French shores, the first word they learn is "strike."

Personally I'm very much in favor of the right to strike. It's one of those fundamental human rights. But sometimes, when I found the post office closed yet again or nobody answered the phone at the airport, I did wish there was a French version of that notorious Californian law: three strikes, and you're out.

36

Bastille Day

Bastille Day is a big national holiday. It commemorates the rebellion in Paris on July 14, 1789, when a mob of citizens threw open the gates of the hated Bastille prison, and released a rather disappointing total of seven political prisoners. This was the beginning of the French revolution, and the beginning of modern France. Today, this mid-July weekend is the peak time for vacation traffic. From then until the end of August, the south of France is absolutely full, standing room only. It was not a bad time to leave.

I've often felt that the French really enjoyed their revolution, chaotic and anarchic though it was. They have never quite got over it. You can tell by the way they drive and park that the spirit of anarchy is not dead. Evading government regulations is practically a patriotic duty. And there's a fierce patriotism that appears on occasions like Bastille Day that makes a foreigner feel just a bit out of place.

At the end of our stay in Aniane, it felt almost like home. The village streets, the stores, the cafés, the people, and the cats had become part of our daily lives, although we never figured out more than a fraction of what was going on. Even the opening and closing times of Monsieur Vidal's general store remained a mystery to the very end. Our neighbors were entirely welcoming, strangers were friendly and helpful, we never felt rejected.

But this was the worst year for Franco-American relations since the Louisiana Purchase. Under the Bush regime America sank back into the most primitive kind of isolationism. The President's rejection of the Kyoto agreement on global warming, the germ warfare treaty, the nuclear non-proliferation agreement, and the International War Crimes Tribunal were seen as direct attacks on Europe in general and France in particular. To add insult to injury, American Lance Armstrong won the favorite French sporting event, the Tour de France, three times in a row—a record that he extended to four times in 2002.

Yet French popular culture was and is obsessed with American themes. Even the distinguished newspaper *Le Monde* crams its pages with reviews of American novels, movies and art. That's why French journalists and intellectuals agonize over the problem of foreign influence and the question of French identity.

In my opinion they have plenty of identity, almost too much. Nobody can be French like the French, or remind you so often that you are *not* French, which they see as a misfortune rather than a fault. But there are some disturbing trends. It's not just movies and McDonalds, but the fact that the most deeply valued part of France, the French heartland or *la France profonde*, has become part of the global real estate marketplace.

It's a pattern repeated all over Europe in attractive villages like Aniane. Newcomers buy and refurbish the romantic old village houses. The original inhabitants, especially the young ones, want nothing more than to move out to a nice villa in the suburbs, or to the nearby city. These migrations create what I call the anachronistic village: church bells and satellite dishes, traditional families living in poverty right next to wealthy professionals from Paris, Berlin, and New York. If you look into the street level windows of the medieval houses of Aniane you might see an old lady knitting in her rocking chair. But you are just as likely to see the glowing icon of Windows 2000. In places like Provence, some of the prettier villages have been more or less completely colonized by outsiders. Ancient stone houses built by and for peasants have acquired proper plumbing, air conditioning, and high-speed Internet connections. The paradoxes multiply.

Where does this leave traditional French culture? The answer seems to be: fighting an energetic rearguard action, and winning, at least some of the time. The drama of our year in Aniane was a David and Goliath battle between the village wine growers and the Californian wine giant Mondavi. This village was chosen by Mondavi for the production of a new prestige wine, requiring a big investment. The locals had mixed feelings about this. But it seemed to be a done deal, until the municipal elections in spring. The old socialist mayor was thrown out of office, and the new communist mayor cancelled the project, claiming that small farmers couldn't survive this kind of competition, and adding that he "Would never accept the presence a big multinational" in his community. So, for the moment, the menace of global capitalism was rolled back, at least in Aniane.

It wasn't quite a new French revolution, but it was definitely in the same rebellious tradition. I don't think we need to worry that our temporary presence in Aniane has polluted the pure stream of French culture. French culture can take care of itself.

THE END

0-595-25337-7